BEING PROPERTY ONCE MYSELF

Being Property Once Myself

Blackness and the End of Man

JOSHUA BENNETT

THE BELKNAP PRESS OF
HARVARD UNIVERSITY PRESS
Cambridge, Massachusetts
London, England

First Harvard University Press paperback edition, 2022
First printing

Library of Congress Cataloging-in-Publication Data
Names: Bennett, Joshua (Poet), author.
Title: Being property once myself : blackness and the end of man / Joshua Bennett.
Description: Cambridge, Massachusetts : The Belknap Press of Harvard University
Press, 2020. | Includes bibliographical references and index.
Identifiers: LCCN 2019040015 (print) | LCCN 2019040016 (ebook) |
ISBN 9780674980303 (cloth) | ISBN 9780674271166 (pbk.)
Subjects: LCSH: Blacks in literature. | American literature—African American
authors—History and criticism. | Literature and race—United States. |
Animals in literature. | Anthropomorphism in literature.
Classification: LCC PS173.N4 B46 2020 (print) | LCC PS173.N4 (ebook) |
DDC 810.9/352996073—dc23
LC record available at https://lccn.loc.gov/2019040015
LC ebook record available at https://lccn.loc.gov/2019040016

for all that persists

CONTENTS

BEING PROPERTY ONCE MYSELF

INTRODUCTION

Horse

> The Negro is America's metaphor.
>
> —Richard Wright

The very first paragraph of Frederick Douglass's 1845 autobiography, *Narrative of the Life of Frederick Douglass,* presents us with a claim that leaps off the page as a problem for modern thought. One rooted in an altogether improper adjacency given the conventions and central aims of the slave narrative as a form, that is, to serve as black humanity's literary proof. Douglass writes, "I was born in Tuckahoe, near Hillsborough, and about twelve miles from Easton, in Talbot County, Maryland. I have no accurate knowledge of my age, never having seen any authentic record containing it. By far the larger part of the slaves know as little of their ages as horses know of theirs."[1] This moment of all-too-fraught proximity between the enslaved black person and the nonhuman animal—positioned here as *twin* captives, affixed by modernity's long arc—demands our attention. What Douglass names is a kinship forged in the midst of unthinkable violence, kinship born of mutual sub-jugation, yes, but also the shared experience of opacity mistaken for emptiness. Here, Douglass foregrounds animal perspective as a means to convey the impossibility of personal history for the en-slaved. A slave's past cannot be recalled because there is no so-cially recognized, generally honored means by which to recall it— no system to record one's emergence into the world, one's entry into the proper chronology, and cosmology, of the human.

Yet one could also argue that Douglass is gesturing toward a deep sense of commonality and even comradeship here. Though the horse is certainly a representative of what is lost, it is also an unlikely ally, one that shares the experience of existing both in-side and outside the parameters of plantation time. The horse is a creature that likewise has no narrative of origin—no chronolog-ical orientation outside its relationship to the slaver's clock—and is thus also constantly moving between the realm of organism and machine, between occupying a space of self-determination and being configured as a *living commodity*. In this sense, horses are, for Douglass, a bridge par excellence between the human and non-human realms. They are saleable, living beings, not unlike Doug-lass and his kin, that are certainly used for labor, entertainment, and breeding but also possess an interiority that is, by the rule, denied.

Douglass forges this unexpected alliance to set up a line of ar-gument that he follows intently throughout the text, a means of getting out of animality *by going through it*. Douglass understands, for example, that under the system of chattel slavery, there are structures in place for the care and sustenance of animals that simply do not exist for the enslaved. As a result, in many of the initial scenes involving horses in Douglass's narrative, there is a confluence of complex emotions: empathy and envy, pity, love, re-sentment and outright rage. Douglass is aware of this unwieldy network of feelings that bind livestock and the enslaved together, and he appears to wrestle at various points with the sadness that emerges from living in such fraught proximity: the contradictions implicit in being asked to care for a creature that is, on many oc-casions, granted more freedom, and more room to move, than one-self. During a speech delivered in 1873 in Nashville, Tennessee, entitled "Agriculture and Black Progress," Douglass takes this point a bit further: "Not only the slave, but the horse, the ox, and the mule shared the general feeling of indifference to rights natu-rally engendered by a state of slavery. . . . The master blamed the overseer; the overseer the slave, and the slave the horses, oxen, and mules; and violence and brutality fell upon animals as a conse-quence."[2] Douglass goes on to entreat his listeners at the time—an audience composed primarily of recently emancipated black farmers—to consider animals their co-laborers, friends, partners in the field, to resist the whims of a social order predicated on their confinement and instead embrace another, more radical form of sociality, one grounded in the desire for a world without cages or chains.

In this sense and others, Douglass's horse embodies the cen-tral concerns of this book. The argument of *Being Property Once Myself: Blackness and the End of Man* is that the overarching claims Douglass is making can be found throughout the African Amer-ican literary tradition. That is, rather than triumphalist rhetoric that would eschew the nonhuman altogether, what we often find instead are authors who envision the Animal as a source of un-fettered possibility, or, to call on the work of John Berger, the Animal as a *promise*.[3] And what does the Animal promise, exactly?

What do black authors create when they are willing to engage in a critical embrace of what has been used against them as a tool of derision and denigration, to leap into a vision of human personhood rooted not in the logics of private property or dominion but in wildness, flight, brotherhood and sisterhood beyond blood?

This book is composed of five chapters, each of which tracks a specific animal figure—the rat, the cock, the mule, the dog, and the shark—in the works of several twentieth- and twenty-first-century writers: Richard Wright, Toni Morrison, Zora Neale Hurston, Jesmyn Ward, and Robert Hayden, respectively. I argue that animal figures are deployed in these texts to assert a theory of black sociality and *black feeling*, as well as to combat certain foundational claims within the Western philosophical tradition broadly construed. My goal throughout this work is to illumine the ways in which the black aesthetic tradition provides us with the tools needed to conceive of interspecies relationships anew and ultimately to abolish the forms of antiblack thought that have maintained the fissure between human and animal. For this too is what W. E. B. Du Bois might have us think of as *the gift* of black culture, the gift of blackness: the great chain of being come undone, life itself unfettered and moving in all directions, a window into the worlds that thrive at the underside of modernity. What does the Animal promise? Nothing short of another cosmos. A radically different set of relations is possible. As Douglass and others demonstrate, such an order is already here, already in the works, already waiting for us in the wild.

This book focuses on the literary imagination and the broader set of ethical concerns that have emerged from African American experiences of living as sociolegal *nonpersons:* a subgenre of the human, always already positioned in fraught proximity to animal

life. Its title is a loving riff on the first two lines of the untitled
Lucille Clifton poem that starts off her 1972 collection *Good News
about the Earth:*

> being property once myself
> i have a feeling for it,
> that's why i can talk
> about environment.
> what wants to be a tree,
> ought to be he can be it.
> same thing for other things.
> same thing for men.[4]

And who is this good news for, exactly? Probably those who know
bad news all too well, those who recognize this offer of a world in
which one can refashion the self at will, find kin among (living)
things, and claim a vision of human personhood rooted not in
ownership but rather in the desire for recognition and care, as a
world that many of us are still waiting on. As is Clifton in so much
of her work, I am interested in the ongoing entanglement of blackness and animality in black social, civic, and psychic life, moments when black people and nonhuman animals are forced to live
in too-close quarters, physical (the plantation, the wilderness, the
kitchenette overrun with pests), legal (the coterminous valuation
and sale of animals and slaves during chattel slavery), or otherwise.
In the midst of such systemic dehumanization, what new ways of
thinking about personhood have emerged? How have black authors cultivated a poetics of persistence and interspecies empathy,
a literary tradition in which nonhuman—and thus also, ostensibly,
nonthinking—life forms are acting up and out in ways we might
not expect or yet have a language for?

For instance, how do we configure Countee Cullen's historically ignored pair of children's books, both coauthored with his cat,
Christopher, within the African American literary tradition?[5]
What do we make of Henry Bibb's explicit, outspoken jealousy of
the freedoms (to take flight, to move freely, to resist capture) that
are enjoyed by snakes and birds but unavailable to the enslaved?[6]
These texts supply us with scenes that are difficult to incorporate
into any triumphalist approach to post-Emancipation black literatures and force us instead to grapple with a different set of questions around what the historical proximity of black people and
nonhuman animals means for how we should read bestial presence
in African American letters.

Though the animating questions of this book can be found long
before the publication of many of the twentieth-century texts that
constitute its core, it is nonetheless in the writings of theorists such
as W. E. B. Du Bois, Gwendolyn Brooks, Jean Toomer, and others
that the intersections I hope to map find their most robust expression. For example, it is Du Bois's theorization of black persons as
tertium quid, "somewhere between men and cattle, . . . a clownish,
simple creature, at times even lovable within its limitations, but
straitly foreordained to walk within the Veil," that motivates much
of my ongoing interest in thinking of black lives as those that are
often positioned outside the human-animal divide altogether and
placed elsewhere in a zone of nonbeing where the kinds of ex-
travagant violence so often deployed against, and solely reserved
for, animals is made allowable, deemed necessary in order for
white civil society to function at peak performance.[7] The nature of
this dual bind—that is, the historical experience of being configured as a not-quite-nonhuman form of life, indeed, as a *human*

nonperson—as well as the body of literature that emerges from within that confinement, is this study's primary concern.

Put differently, this project emerges from the uneasy collision of mourning and celebration, and derives its force from the meditative tenacity of authors willing to turn to the animal kingdom, that which had so often been used as a tool of their derision and punishment, as a site of futurity and fugitivity. This is a refusal rooted in the knowledge that, as Audre Lorde reminds us, "we were never meant to survive." Not only a celebration in spite of antiblack structures of feeling, or a capitalist order predicated on the wanton destruction of nonhuman forms of life, but a kind that employs those conditions as the very grounds for a divergent mode of being in the world.[8] If black people and animals are co-constructed as living flesh but never as *bodies*, then what protective protocols might black authors have cultivated to celebrate the flesh, to love it as Baby Suggs, herself a physically disabled field hand who is characterized at one point in Toni Morrison's *Beloved* as "a sixty-odd-year-old slavewoman who walks like a three-legged dog," implores us to?[9] Often, I will argue, loving blackness comes at a high price and is almost always linked to a refutation of the human as the only form of life worthy of mourning or ethical engagement.

What these authors appear to be seeking, alongside the space to be properly grieved—which is to say, to be recognized as not already dead in every way that matters—is a vision of life that is profoundly *ecological*, one that takes place in a social field made up of dynamic relationships not predicated solely on domination or exploitation. In this sense, their work is extending and elaborating on what Michel Serres has termed, in contradistinction to a social contract, a *natural contract*, a way of imagining interplay across species that foregrounds "symbiosis and reciprocity," a contract "in which our relationship to things would set aside mastery and possession in favor of admiring attention, reciprocity, contemplation, and respect: where knowledge would no longer imply property, nor action mastery."[10] Through a collective envisioning of the natural contract that doubles as a theory of blackness—which is also to say, a theory of gender and a theory of *genre*—these authors open up space for something like a fundamentally *black ecology*, an explosion of the limits imposed by a disciplinary or otherwise aversion to thinking with nonhuman forms of life at the level of the psychic, the literary, and the sociopolitical.[11]

I will argue that it is precisely this commitment to engaging with the fullness of nonhuman animal worlds, as well as a profound wrestling with what it means to live in a social matrix in which one is cast as a lower order of organism, that demands sustained critical attention. Such a history begs the question, How does one delight in a precarious life? What useful blues might we find in an archive full of folks forced to write against perpetual misrecognition? My argument will be that these authors, writing as they are against centuries of dehumanizing discourse made material in law, literature, and various instances of everyday inequality, are able to articulate a set of ethics, and what is more, a philosophy of mind, that is instructive for those of us interested in thinking toward a more robust vision of human, and nonhuman, cognitive and otherwise potential in the contemporary moment. By engaging in extensive close readings of the scenes in which nonhuman animals appear in twentieth- and twenty-first-century African American literature, I hope to expound on the counterhegemonic, and also seemingly *counterintuitive*, ways that black authors often render animal life in their poetry and fiction. I am primarily interested in how animal figures are deployed therein in order to make arguments about the nature of black sociality, black interiority, and *black feeling*, as well as to combat certain foundational claims within the Western philosophical tradition regarding the limits and lacunae of personhood broadly construed.

I imagine this book as an interdisciplinary project firmly situated at the nexus of black studies, ecocriticism and affect theory. This particular ensemble of fields fits well together given my desire to examine both what is happening at the level of direct action in each text and how these texts might operate individually and in concert as toolkits for thinking about the workings of antiblackness, and the black social and political imagination that strains against it, in the material world. The book is, in this respect, both a survey and an extended meditation on a particular historical phenomenon, both an account of the ongoing animalization of black peoples within a contemporary US context and a gesture toward how we might trace the effects and affects of this particular species of antiblack racism across space and time, placing it in conversation with a wide spectrum of responses from within the universe of black letters.

There are few scholars who have pulled these divergent, and largely nascent, fields together for the purposes of a larger project. Nevertheless, there are a number of contemporary theorists with whom this book is in direct conversation, including Fred Moten, Hortense Spillers, Evie Shockley, Kimberly N. Ruffin, Ian Finseth, Paul Outka, Zakkiyah Jackson, Camille Dungy, and Michael Lundblad. Each of these thinkers' work reflects a robust engagement across both field and genre that this book seeks to emulate, especially as it pertains to unsettling familiar categories (for example, "the animal" or "the body"). In the current landscape of literary theory, this book is entering much-larger conversations currently taking place around new materialisms, animal ethics, and the intractability of antiblack violence in our historical moment. In that vein, several academic texts have recently been released that accomplish something like the transversal analysis of antiblackness and animalization that I am interested in pursuing in this book. Spanning genre and period, each of these texts stands in one way or another as a cogent critique of the ways in which these connections have heretofore been mapped in animal studies, ecocriticism, and black studies alike.

The first text of interest in this group Camille Dungy's fantastic anthology *Black Nature: Four Centuries of African-American Nature Poetry*, a book that served in many ways as my own entrée into the subgenre of black nature writing and pushed me from early on to think both historically and thematically about how specific animals might be operating in African American texts at the level of trope. Taken in its totality, *Black Nature* represents the best of what one might hope for when handling the sort of historical materials I am interested in: a collection of poetry and prose that neither obscures the horrors of racism and animalization nor traffics in a too-neat sense of collective overcoming or inevitable jubilee. What *Black Nature* does instead is wrestle with the always already fraught character of certain encounters between blacks and animals, inviting us to admire the beauty of the open without ever losing ourselves in the notion that the category of the human has a kind of coherence or inclusiveness built into it.

Kimberley N. Ruffin's *Black on Earth: African American Literary Connections* and Michael Lundblad's *Birth of a Jungle: Animality in Progressive Era U.S. Literature and Culture* approach the gap in the literary historical archive much differently than *Black Nature* does, both relying primarily on a combination of literary fiction and historical materials to make their cases, respectively, for (1) rethinking the historical relationship between black thinkers and US American ecological discourse and (2) forging a line of flight away from something like animal studies in order to engage in what Lundblad terms *animality studies,* an intellectual project centrally concerned with the ways in which certain kinds of organic life become animalized through law and literature.

Another text that is in direct conversation with this book is Marjorie Spiegel's controversial book *The Dreaded Comparison: Human and Animal Slavery,* which focuses primarily on the sites of overlap between chattel slavery in the Americas in the seventeenth century and what she terms *animal slavery:* the ongoing capture and slaughter of nonhuman animals worldwide for the sake of human consumption, recreation, and profit. Though I am interested in many of the same *historical* intersections as Spiegel is, my ultimate aim is not to place chattel slavery and the exploitation of nonhuman animals side by side as a means of highlighting the ostensibly undertheorized plight of nonhuman animals so much as to investigate the ways in which animal life operates as a site of recognition and reckoning for African American authors in the twentieth century and beyond.

Where this book will differ from these existing works is that my earliest objects of inquiry are firmly situated within the confines of the twentieth and twenty-first centuries. I imagine this project as the next step in a logical progression from many of the texts I have outlined herein not only in the sense of chronology but also at the level of genre. I also want to note that while there are other books and articles that take up the relationship between black people and the natural world as their subject matter, there are none I have come across that pay extensive attention to the specific set of relations that interest me, that is, the ways in which literary encounters between black folks and various forms of animal life in twentieth- and twenty-first-century literature provide us with alternative models for thinking blackness and personhood *as such* in the present day.

Finally, I want to note that the subtitle of this book, *Blackness and the End of Man*, is an inheritance from the Jamaican theorist, playwright, dancer, poet, and novelist Sylvia Wynter. Directly in line with the larger sociopolitical, and semiotic, problem of Man as an *overrepresentation of the human*, I have attempted here to offer an alternative vision of the human through the lens of black literary studies. My argument throughout this book is that the vision of personhood offered by various writers in the black aesthetic tradition represents a response to both a Hegelian account of personhood, in which "the person has for its substantive end the right of placing its will in any and every thing,"[12] and to a variant of personhood established and enforced by contemporary jurisprudence, in which "not every human being is necessarily a person, for a person is capable of rights and duties, and there may well be human beings having no legal rights, as was the case with slaves in English law. . . . A person is such not *because he is human*, but because rights and duties are ascribed to him."[13]

For those who have historically not been able to, or simply not *desired* to, exert their will in things but have instead had to count themselves as both among and *as infinitely more than things*, there have always been other approaches to imagining how they might love and live in their flesh, as well as *what they might call* such living. In response to this lived experience of moving through the material world without the legal rights ascribed to the ostensibly autonomous, rights-bearing, legal person—what Wynter's oeuvre shows us is actually the figure of Man, masquerading as the only viable genre of the human person—African American authors have, from the very beginning, envisioned and enacted alternative ways of being human and thinking human personhood. This book is my attempt to map that fugitive practice, that black love that enters the world in and through and as literary study, as it appears in the figure of the animal. This mapping is inextricable from Wynter's call, especially in her later writings and interviews, for a serious reconsideration of the importance of *origin stories* in the field of black studies and elsewhere.[14]

This book is an initial gesture toward the larger project of reconsidering the origins of the field of black literary studies, as well as a revision and a re-envisioning of the sites at which something like black literary study might be said to take place, what sorts of unwieldy, largely unthought forms of interspecies collaboration, convergence, and conviviality might be involved in such an undertaking. If antiblackness is the weather, as Christina Sharpe writes, then perhaps black study, black sociality, black care, and laughter in our life behind the Veil is our way of moving through it, around it, below it.[15] Perhaps it is, in some sense, our ark, our simultaneous shelter from the storm and vessel bound for elsewhere. What does black thought in the end times, at the End of Man, look like? Strangers gathered in the Clearing, perhaps, to envisage a new way. A loving glance. New language that might honor where we are now, where we have been, and the places we are going that we cannot yet imagine.

❀

Chapter 1 will focus on the role of rats in the poetry and fiction of Richard Wright. Though Wright's singular focus on the sustained threat of violent death that permeates black presence in the public sphere—as well as what such an ongoing imposition makes of black interior life and the possibility of black sociality—is undertheorized within contemporary literary theory, what has received even less scholarly attention are the ways in which Wright's commitment to thinking about black death is mediated through the appearance and activity of nonhuman animals, most frequently, and most germane to this chapter, the figure of the pest.[16] Indeed, an abundance of pest animals populate Wright's work, but it is the rat that animates the scenes in his poetry and fiction that most clearly articulate his relationship to black suffering as well as black persistence, its hunger and spirited refusal to be captured that best characterize the way he portrays the persons who are most central to the concerns of this study: Bigger Thomas and the anonymous speaker of his nature haiku. It is my goal, then, through an extended reading of the opening scene of Wright's most famous novel, *Native Son*, to interrogate the way Wright imagines black life through the figure of the pest instead of against it, crafting characters that are consistently under duress but also always in flight, always fugitive from forces seen and unseen that depend on their subjugation for life.

Chapter 2 is centrally concerned with the uses of the black masculine in Toni Morrison's *Song of Solomon*. Therein, I argue, Morrison's emphasis on the presence and, most importantly, the *properties* of animals is notably gendered and provides a fertile ground for imagining a theory of the black masculine grounded in literary analysis. Put differently, I am interested here in the ways in which Morrison uses animals, and birds in particular, to make a certain argument about how it *feels* to be a black man, how she uses them in order not only to critique the limiting, violent ways in which black masculinity is structured *from the outside* but to describe the means through which black men and boys bear such weight, how they comport themselves under the duress of everyday life as a perceived threat. Following Afaa Weaver's suggestion that "black men are the summary of weight," Chapter 2 tracks the way that black masculinity as heaviness, as excess, as impediment, as vanity, as *exorbitance* moves through *Song of Solomon* in the bodies of birds, how these animals, rather paradoxically, come to signal a certain boundedness to earth, an unwieldy abundance that limits all possibility of mobility, escape, or futurity.[17] Alongside Nahum Chandler and others, however, I would like to think imaginatively about what such exorbitance avails to us as a frame for imagining alternative black masculinities and to begin with the premise of abundance rather than absence.

For the purposes of Chapter 3, I am interested in how Zora Neale Hurston's uses of the figure of the mule might elucidate new pathways for thinking at the intersections of blackness, animality, and gender, how her persistent emphasis on the disparate kinds of violation, silencing, and suppression that circumscribe black women's everyday experiences—especially when such violation is juxtaposed against spectacular scenes of violence against non-human animals and explicitly linked to the experience of those animals by the text's central characters—helps us to think not only about muleness as a critical agent in *Their Eyes Were Watching God* but about the mule as a figure of central importance in the field of black feminist thought. Further, in this chapter I seek to illuminate the ways in which a critical engagement with muleness opens up a number of different avenues through which we might approach *Their Eyes Were Watching God* as a part of Hurston's broader corpus, in which bestial presence is always already an irruptive force to be reckoned with. I intend for this chapter to reflect the inherent *multiplicity* of muleness as a means of indexing value, which is also to say, the indeterminate, uncanny workings of the black feminine in a text that is deeply concerned with how we might read persistence, even abundance, in spaces and, most centrally, onto *forms of human and nonhuman life* that are traditionally marked as nonsites, as vitalized forms of death.[18] It is precisely this critical practice of valuing black and nonhuman life, over and against dominant ways of thinking about or assigning such value, that, I will argue, is what Hurston wants us to consider when muleness enters the frame.

Chapter 4 will focus primarily on the role of dogs in Jesmyn Ward's 2011 novel *Salvage the Bones*. To open, I will undertake a close reading of Carl Philips's poem "White Dog," in an effort to see what happens when the immediate threat of violence is removed from a poem that contains all of the other elements that have heretofore been discussed as mediating factors in the relationship between black people and dogs. I proceed to engage in an extended reading of *Salvage the Bones*, with special emphasis on the ways in which motherhood is marshaled by Ward in order to unsettle normative, anthropocentric modes of imagining kinship and relation more broadly. By crafting a constellation of human and nonhuman actors that are all explicitly marked as mothers, I argue that Ward demands that the reader relinquish the impulse to flatten motherhood into solely a space of nurturing or care and embrace a much more troubled, and troubling, view, one that fully engages with the violence of the natural world, as well as the gratuitous, ostensibly *unnatural* violence imposed by the regulatory forces of a white-supremacist social order.

Chapter 5 explores the uses of sharks in twentieth- and twenty-first-century African American poetry. How does the ever-present specter of the transatlantic slave trade—what we might think of, following Saidiya Hartman and other critics, as the afterlife of slavery—propel us to theorize black ecopoetics not as a matter of *ground* but as an occasion to think at the intersection of terra firma and open sea, surface and benthos, the observable ocean and the uncharted blackness of its very bottom? Given recent critical attention paid to African American nature writing, I am interested in how we might think alongside black writers who have historically taken up oceanic ecology, and their necessarily strained relationship to it, as a central concern. Specifically, in this chapter I will concentrate on the writings of two major twentieth-century African American poets, Robert Hayden and Melvin Tolson, in order to elaborate a theory of black ecopoetics gone offshore. I will undertake this project primarily through investigating the ways that both poets deploy sharks in their writings about the long historical reach of antiblackness as a dominant structure of feeling, as well as the ongoing presence of black persistence and black fugitive possibility.

I

Rat

———

The question is whether such likening of the "other human" ends only in similitude or whether it authorizes, operationalizes, and becomes an ethics toward such labeled humans. In short, what are the material consequences of relegation from human being to vermin being (a pest or nuisance that must be eliminated)? The term *pesticide* might be innovatively used to encompass not only the substances used to kill pests but also the theory and practice of killing them. . . . Vermin (the nonhuman) are not only pests to be controlled but also actors that coproduce and impact their wouldbe controllers. . . . Since Daniel Headrick's *Tools of Empire* and Alfred Crosby's *Ecological Imperialism,* studies that follow the itineraries of Europeans and "things European"— technology, science, microbes, and so on—explain what Europeans did but not what these vermin beings "did back."

—Clapperton Chakanetsa Mavhunga, "Vermin Beings:
On Pestiferous Animals and Human Game"

I was on my way to a life of bagging tiny mountains,
selling poetry on the corners of North Philly,
a pest to mothers & Christians.
Hearing it too the cop behind me shoved me
aside for he was an entomologist
in a former lifetime & knew the many

song structures of cicadas, bush crickets &
fruit flies. He knew the complex courtship
of bark beetles, how the male excavates
a nuptial chamber & buries himself,
his back end sticking out till a female sang
a lyric of such intensity he squirmed like a Quaker
& gave himself over to the quiet history
of trees & ontology. All this he said while
patting me down, slapping first my ribs, then
sliding his palms along the sad, dark shell
of my body

—Major Jackson, "Pest"

Another federal lawsuit filed in 2003 by the Housing Rights
Center and 19 tenants accused [former Los Angeles Clippers
owner Donald] Sterling of once stating his preference not to
rent to Latinos because "Hispanics smoke, drink and just hang
around the building." The lawsuit also accused him of saying
"black tenants smell and attract vermin."

—"Clippers Owner Is No Stranger to Race-Related Lawsuits,"
Los Angeles Times

Though Richard Wright's singular focus on the sustained threat of violent death that permeates black presence in the public sphere—as well as what such an ongoing imposition makes of black interior life and the possibility of black sociality—is undertheorized within contemporary literary theory, what has received even less scholarly attention are the ways in which Wright's commitment to thinking about black death is mediated through the appearance and activity of animals, most frequently and most germane to this study, the figure of the pest.[1] In the interest of precision, some clarification of terms is in order:

The Oxford English Dictionary defines a pest as: "Any thing or person that is noxious, destructive or troublesome." A variety of other definitions exist in the biological literature, as for example: "a living organism which causes damage or illness to Man or his possessions or is otherwise in some sense, 'unwanted,'" . . . but most biological definitions include some consideration of the economic significance of the damage caused. Thus "A pest is an organism which harms Man or his property or is likely to do so. The harm must be significant, the damage of economic importance." . . . This last distinction is I feel an important one: much time and effort has been devoted in the past to the control of animal populations whose activities, while doubtless of considerable nuisance value were perhaps, if the situation were viewed more objectively, of no real economic significance. In such situations costs of control quite frequently exceed the real costs of any damage caused.[2]

This selection from R. J. Putnam's 1934 text *Mammals as Pests* is instructive for my own study in its engagement with the many resonances of the term "pest," especially as they pertain to questions of value. As Putnam makes clear, part of what qualifies a pest as such is that it by definition carries along with its body the perceived threat of economic loss or damage. It is this very characteristic that makes the pest a source of its danger and its life altogether disposable, that is, the animal's destructive orientation toward civil society and the structures, material and otherwise, that keep it intact. There is a fundamental conundrum built into this relationship, however, one that Putnam wastes little time in pointing out: more often than not, the very processes deployed in service of terminating pest animals come at a higher financial cost than the initial damage incurred or the overall damage projected. Put differently, the central problem that the pest poses is undoubtedly *economic;* it just has little to do with money. For Putnam, the wages of pestiferous life are the toll that pests take on the psychic economy of a given space, the cost to an inhabitant of letting live what does not belong, what invades or remains though it is unwanted. By virtue of its very presence, the pest puts immense pressure on the integrity of wherever it chooses to take up room, slowly sapping the sense of propriety or private ownership that a given owner might lay claim to. Such an interruption, through the screen door, cabinet, or kitchen sink, is also always already an irruption into the logic of private property, an untenable counter to anthropocentric conceptions of human domination and domesticity.

Pests destroy the myth of private property from the inside out, though it is not solely for this reason that they are so often made into objects of state violence and/or hailed as a threat to public health. Such reasoning often comes back instead to the threat that pests pose to the possibility of a self-contained human subjectivity, one that thrives on a certain distance from contact or contamination. A home without pests is a home in which one can ostensibly live without threat of sickness or stolen food, the sorts of everyday risks that are all too familiar to those who are made to live without sufficient shelter. In this sense, pests not only defamiliarize the logic of private property but also wage war on traditional ideas of inside and outside. In "Feeling Animal: Pet-Making and Mastery in the *Slave's Friend*," Spencer D. C. Keralis writes,

> Pets largely do not provide a service in the household but rather
> fulfill aesthetic and emotional needs for their masters. (The benefit to the pet is arguable.) Cats and dogs that serve as mousers

and ratters sometimes blur this distinction, but more often a household in which animals are kept for these purposes will also include house pets not used for labor. The services provided by mousers and ratters connect them in the minds of their nominal owners to the feral origin of their species, and the killing of vermin causes them to be perceived as unsanitary. They are excluded from the domestic sphere as "outside dogs" or "barn cats," though sporting dogs used for hunting can be exceptions to this rule.[3]

According to Keralis, what is most contagious about pest animals is not any microscopic biological agent but their very nature, that which marks them as outsiders. The pest transmogrifies all that it touches—even those animals charged solely with its elimination or curtailment—into a filthy thing that has no place within the domestic sphere. In this way, the pest serves as a marker of alterity, its presence in a given space a trustworthy indicator of what goes on therein, what class or kind of person calls the room between such filthy walls home. I would like to argue that it is this central concern with the contagious alterity of the pest that accounts for much of the violence deployed in its direction, the prevalent notion that, beyond the level of disease and discomfort, pests carry with them a disrepute that is largely incurable.

Thus, it is the central fiction of pesticide, the hunting and killing of pests solely as a practice of maintenance, cleanliness, or fiscal thrift, that is of special concern here, how it is that such violence can be waged under the auspices of austerity while coming at such great financial and ethical cost. If we understand pestiferous life as that which is fundamentally disposable, as so repugnant that it must be destroyed even when such erasure garners a high price, then what happens when we expand the category to include human lives? What social and material conditions allow for such a gratuitous marring of the human person? What makes it so that the province of the human can be so easily split between those that are allowed to flourish and those whose lives are made legible only in contrast to something like public life or citizenship, those that must be wiped out for the comfort and care of those in power?

Richard Wright's larger corpus can be cast in one light as an extended meditation on such questions, and the figure of the pest serves as an especially effective tool in his argument for a reading of black social life as that which is always already marked by a certain orientation toward danger. Indeed, Wright's central metaphor for thinking black life after the Great Migration is no noble beast, neither the oxen nor the horse that we see in early black literature's forays into the plantation, but the figure par excellence of disposable life and thus also of black domestic life in the urban context: the rat. Though an abundance of pest animals populate Wright's work, it is the rat that animates the scenes in his poetry and fiction that most clearly articulate his relationship to black suffering as well as black persistence, its hunger and spirited refusal to be captured that best characterize the way he portrays the persons most central to the concerns of this study: Bigger Thomas and the anonymous speaker of his nature haiku.

It is my goal, then, through an extended reading of the opening scene of Wright's most famous novel, *Native Son*, to interrogate the way he imagines black life through the figure of the pest instead of against it, crafting characters that are consistently under duress but also always in flight, always fugitive from forces seen and unseen that depend on their subjugation for life. For Wright, black persistence is not a site of celebration so much as an occasion for melancholy, a reminder that the world that he and his kin strain against is as tireless as it is resourceful. Working from such a vantage point, he provides his readers with characters that both encounter pest animals and live into a kind of pestiferous life themselves that is full of unfettered possibility. In Wright's hands, the pest is not only that which is stalked by death but that which evades it, that which destabilizes life and death altogether, giving us something in its place akin to fugitive life, black life on the lam.

In an effort to better understand the opening scene of *Native Son* within the broader scope of its historical and material context, as well as to more imaginatively examine the ways in which Wright's particular emphasis on the rat as a kind of pest animal par excellence travel throughout the African American literary canon— even into the contemporary moment—the following section of a poem by Tara Betts, "For Those Who Need a True Story" (here quoted at length), is invaluable:

> The landlord told Raymond's mother that twelve dollars
> would be deducted from the rent for every rat killed.
> She sends her son to the store for a loaf of Wonder Bread
> and five pounds of ground beef. Young Raymond
> returns with bread & meat that she tears & mixes inside
> a metal bowl. Mama seasons the meatloaf with rat poison
> pulled from the cabinet beneath the sink. Well done,
> meat sits steaming in the middle of the kitchen floor.
> Then the scratching scurries. The squeaking begins
> and screeches toward the bowl.

Raymond describes the wave of rats like a tidal crash
covering the bow, leaping over each other's bodies
then the dropping, the stutter kicks.

A chorus of rat screams ramble through Raymond's ears.
Keening, furry bodies tense paws against churning guts
as they hit cracked linoleum until an hour passes.
Silence swept away the din in death's footsteps.
The mother's voice quivers in her next request.
Raymond, help me count them.[4]

What Betts's poem brings to the fore—and it is important to note
here that Betts, like Wright, spent much of her adult life in Chicago
and sets a scene for us that could easily be imagined as something akin to the South Side kitchenette that serves as this chapter's central focus—are alternative possibilities for thinking the
relationship between blacks and pest animals in domestic space,
one in which the symbolism of pestiferous life lies not in its like-
ness to black ontology but rather in the problem of its sheer abundance, an infestation of rats so severe that their very dying might
be described as a "tidal crash" that lasts for so long that Raymond
and his mother have to sit together, away from the chaos, "until
an hour passes."

The prevalence of rats in the apartment that Raymond and his
mother share is not a reflection of the worth that they place on
their own lives—indeed, the very planning of this elaborate killing
by Raymond's mother demonstrates a love and depth of care that
should be central to any reading of this poem—but could be said
to reflect the disposition of the landlord who makes the wager that
serves as the poem's first line and guiding conflict. It is the lack of
value that an antiblack world places on Raymond's and his mother's

lives that creates the conditions for this precarious living, these unwieldy experiments undertaken so that either of them might get
through a night without being bitten. In the world that Betts con-
structs, rats are still representational in a sense, but in a very different way than they are for someone like Wright or any number
of other black poets who have used the persona poem as a means
of entering the body of the pest, taking up its struggle, and imagining their own experience as racialized subjects as akin to vermin
being.[5] What we get here instead is a set of scenes that are no less
radical or daring, a work in which Betts dares to lay out the kind
of violence that such predatory forms of capitalism inflict on black
families living at the edge of the civil. In "For Those Who Need a
True Story," rats become the only way out of an otherwise impos-
sible situation, a means through which Raymond and his mother
might plot an escape from unlivable space:

> They waded through these small deaths with rubber gloves,
> listened to the hump of each dead rat as it rustled against
> the slackness of plastic bags.
> Raymond wanted to stop counting,
> but mama needed to save a dozen dollars
> wherever she could
> if they wanted to finally leave the rats behind.
>
> After the last rat was counted, Raymond handed
> The bag to the landlord as proof. *Here.*
>
> Enough rats to skip the rent for three months.
> Enough rats to avoid the fear of sweet sleeping
> breath leading to bitten lips.
> Healthy children wrapped in designer dictates

Cannot describe Raymond's fear of rabies,
The smell of poison rotting from the inside out,
the scratching inside the walls at night.

Those children
Should find soft lives
That drop pendulums in their dreams
And never tell another story
About the ghetto
Until they've had to count rats
With their hands.[6]

In grand fashion, the poem's final stanzas unveil the broader logic behind its central action: Raymond's mother had not planned on getting a discount on rent for the purposes of remaining in the apartment but with an eye toward leaving it altogether. Thus, what originally appeared to be a bargaining chip (the dead rats in exchange for cheaper rent so that the family might remain in the apartment long term) is revealed to be a first step toward flight, the dead rats serving as the only available means by which Raymond's mother might actualize a different life for her family. Betts's final gesture toward the ways in which stories like that of Raymond and his mother are put under erasure in favor of more palatable ideas about what it might mean to inhabit a "true story"—which, as presented here, is inextricable from the tropes of cultural authenticity produced in a marketplace that places great value on one's ability to effectively narrate black suffering—is a move that jars upon first read, both because of its deviation from the mode of the rest of the poem, and also in that it serves as a compelling moment of insight into how the author demands its content be approached.

For Betts, there is another kind of violence that runs alongside the everyday danger of Raymond's and his mother's lives, the ongoing appropriation of such experiences without any engagement with what the material consequences of such living might be. Betts's warning about a contemporary reading public's attraction to the violence of urban living spaces, especially when such an obsession requires no personal investment or material presence, is instructive. What Betts demands is risk, cost, an ethics of engagement that understands "the true story" as that which makes something new and altogether different of the person who experiences it, that which shapes those who live out its strands as forms of knowledge that they carry with them long after the moment recedes into the archive. The true story here is one that is necessarily bound up with the historical weight of the way poor black folks in Chicago have always lived, a history attended to with great care by thinkers such as Sylvia Washington, whose 2005 text *Packing Them In: An Archaeology of Environmental Racism in Chicago, 1865–1954* articulates this last point with clarity and force:

> Despite the midcentury Civil Rights Movement and the Environmental Justice Movement, the majority of Chicago blacks still live in highly racially segregated communities that carry a disproportionate amount of environmental waste disposal facilities. . . . The perception and treatment of blacks under segregationist policies fits Mary Poovey's thesis of the construction of social bodies by those in power in order to isolate a segment of the larger society with the ultimate objectives of managing, manipulating, or controlling them. . . . African Americans living in Chicago throughout the migration period were highly visible and thought of as being a "diseased" segment by the larger social

body and body politic. The aggressive actions by the larger white social body to keep them essentially spatially and environmentally quarantined would lead to violence in the form of race riots and bombings, and, eventually, to de facto segregation.[7]

Following Washington, one can read Betts's poem as in conversation with a much longer history of systemic exclusion and state control leveraged against poor black Chicagoans since the turn of the twentieth century. Read in such a context, Raymond and his mother's collective labor toward escaping their apartment becomes a story not only of individual survival and initiative but of resistance against specific forms of state-sponsored subjugation. The poem's central action doubles as an act of opposition that seeks to undermine the very system of relations that put them in that tenement in the first place, the same system that counts them as but so many expendable bodies. Their escape can thus be read as an act of insurgence, a pushing back against the psychic onslaught of a system of relations in which the lines between home and war are always already blurred, always marred beyond recognition by grime or fire. Over and against such overwhelming structural inequity, the characters that Betts creates nonetheless seek out a better home, regarding the figure of the pest not solely as a natural enemy or obstacle but as a means through which they might seek out a safer home.

Part of what makes Betts's poem so critical to the theoretical considerations that are most germane to this study is that much of my interest in the relationship between blacks and pests is rooted in moments when the figure of the black is *inextricably* linked to the pest animal, when blackness and vermin being are yoked together within a literary scene or the social field itself. These occasions, when the dehumanizing powers of white supremacy and antiblackness operate with such force that black bodies are rendered altogether disposable and deserving of extermination, are plentiful within my archive, but they are not all that persists there. There are also stories like that of Raymond and his mother, whose relationship to pest animals could be called normative if not for the complicated nexus of relations within which their decision to kill and collect the rats in their apartment takes place. The violence they leverage against vermin is not rooted in the dominant logic described by Washington, but in an altogether different sort of conflict than has largely been explored within the realm of animal studies as a field of knowledge production and ongoing critique of human-animal relation.

❁

Unlike the primal scene in Betts's poem, the reader is allowed no distance from the carnage in the opening scene of Wright's masterwork. Our first encounter with the family of Bigger Thomas is one marked by jeering and blood:

> Bigger aimed and let the skillet fly with a heavy grunt. There was a shattering of wood as the box caved in. The woman screamed and hid her face in her hands. Bigger tiptoed forward and peered. "I got 'im," he muttered, his clenched teeth bared in a smile. "By God, I got 'im." He kicked the splintered box out of the way and the flat black body of the rat lay exposed, its two long yellow tusks showing distinctly. Bigger took a shoe and pounded the rat's head, crushing it, cursing hysterically: "You sonofabitch!" The woman on the bed sank to her knees and buried her face in the quilts and sobbed. . . . "Bigger take 'im out" Vera begged. . . .

Bigger laughed and approached the bed with the dangling rat, swinging it to and fro like a pendulum, enjoying his sister's fear.[8]

Though the scene opens with Bigger's killing of the rat, ostensibly in protection of his family members and / or as a means of making their shared domestic space more livable, by the passage's end Bigger's small-scale act of extermination is exposed for what it is: force exerted for his own delight and devoid of any underlying, altruistic motivation. Bigger's aim is to deploy suffering in as many directions as possible, torturing his younger sister with the rat's body as soon as it becomes available for such use.

Consider too the numerous micro-performances that attend Bigger's killing of the rat. The heavy grunt when the skillet first leaves his hands, the smile he bares once it becomes clear that his weapon of choice has served its purpose. From the beginning, that Bigger Thomas derives unmitigated joy from the domination of others, irrespective of age or species, is abundantly clear. What is less apparent is how Bigger imagines he would fair against a target of greater size or strength, one he might not be so quick to attack for fear of retribution or embarrassment. In this moment, Bigger is a character beyond our immediate empathic reach, one that rejoices in the exacerbated killing of a rat—going so far even to mutilate it further with a blunt object once it is already dead—and then taunts his sister with its deceased, bleeding body. To sit with the gruesome nature of this opening scene is to wrestle with many of the central questions of *Native Son* as a whole, questions of socialization and individual choice, a grappling at the level of the act of reading itself with what it means to spend 400 pages with a character capable of such violence and no discernible impetus other than the world we share, a world in which the argument that young men like Bigger are nothing less than ubiquitous flows too easily off the tongues of writers and policy makers alike. Wright, fully aware of such psychic resonances, nonetheless develops a protagonist who lives into that world's worst fears, its most dangerous tropes, and in the process provides a glimpse into the depths of the antiblack public imagination.

In a similar vein, although the way that animality (specifically as it pertains to the inextricability of animality and violence) works thematically in this passage might appear readily obvious—that is, Bigger's literal killing of the rat as a symbolic gesture toward the disposability of animal life, as well as the poor conditions in which city-dwelling black families of his era were forced to live—I would like to draw attention to a number of other, subtler ways that the pest animal registers here not merely as an object of sentiment or identification for the reader, nor solely as an explanatory apparatus for the cruelty we will see from Bigger later in the novel, but indeed as a means through which Bigger himself comes to be animalized. This happens in two distinct ways, the first of which requires us to think of the moment of animalization as not simply an instance in which a human being is literally or figuratively transformed into the equivalent of an animal but also the process *by and through which such metamorphosis takes place*. Put differently, I am interested not only in moments when such a transformation is complete or successful but in the very mechanism of disaggregating human personhood itself, in how and why certain human persons come to have their personhood revoked and what such a theft, at the level of social standing and relation, ultimately makes of their life chances. This distinction is critical in the case of the Bigger Thomas, as the primary way in which he is animalized in *Native Son* is not through the figure of the pest, per se, but in re-

lation to it. It is indeed the *improper* nature of the relationship between Bigger and the rat of the opening scene that marks his ever-
present distance from the human, relegating him to a different space
altogether, that of "the savage," as Michael Lundblad argues:

> Between Darwin and Freud, . . . after the end of the "peculiar in-
> stitution" of slavery in the United States, dominant discourses
> attempted to sidestep . . . evolutionary narrative, suggesting in-
> stead that white men could indeed be linked more closely with
> "the animal" than "the savage" in terms of both "animal instincts"
> and common animal ancestors. A related—but less explored—
> move to distinguish between "civilized" white men and "savage"
> black men was to focus specifically on the treatment of "real" ani-
> mals. Rather than delighting in torture, the civilized man could
> supposedly be identified by the capacity for treating not just
> humans but also animals "humanely." This . . . discourse of
> human reform was born at the same moment that constructions
> of black men were also shifting, and, more specifically an explo-
> sion of lynchings was being justified by the myth of the black
> male rapist, which linked an assault on white womanhood with
> a savage delight in torture. Human reform actually became a new
> and flexible discourse for claiming superiority over various human
> "races," reinforcing the logic that only the more "civilized" group
> had evolved enough to treat other groups "humanely."[9]

Instead of serving as a kind of counter-representation, or straining
against such assumptions about the workings and limitations of
black men's affective imaginations, Wright forwards a figure that
fits rather neatly into such a schema. Bigger does indeed "delight
in torture," as he relishes both the killing of the rat itself and the
sort of cruel teasing of his sister that its death makes possible. This

decision on Wright's behalf, to craft a character whose every action would either run counter to the palate of a respectable white readership or confirm its worst suspicions is one that is well documented both by scholars of Wright and by Wright himself. But beyond such surface correlations between Bigger's depiction and what Wright imagined a white reading audience's reaction to such a depiction might be, it is worth noting that distancing Bigger from this particular discourse around humaneness, at bottom, also does the work of destabilizing the discourse itself. By opening the novel with a scene of such intense violence, one that immediately alienates the reader from Bigger and momentarily interrupts the potential for empathy or a certain kind of mirroring, Wright entreats us to do away with such limited ways of distributing value or personhood, to instead approach the protagonist he has created on his own terms.

To read *Native Son* is to encounter the inner life of a character that muddles such modes of reading and relation and in doing so entreats the reader to ask what compels anyone to hold fast to such categories in the first instance. Taking into account Lundblad's historical treatment of the discourse of humaneness and its relationship to the treatment of animals, what becomes readily obvious is that such thinking is at its very core invested not only in numerous falsehoods about black interior life but also in what the treatment of animals signifies in regard to one's comportment in and toward the social world. In the scenario Lundblad lays out here, the very people marking the various distinctions between humane and inhumane persons are those who themselves benefit from material inequality and structural violence against black human beings. That such a way of thinking about animal treatment obscures the subjugation of black people is central to how we might imagine what Wright's work makes possible for us in the present, a critique of those branches of contemporary animal ethics that bear an uncanny resemblance to what Lundblad gestures toward in the quoted passage, writings where antiblackness is put under complete erasure, removed from the chain of being altogether in favor of a social hierarchy in which white men are the sole actors.

In such a scheme, animals become either objects to be protected by white citizens from nonwhite savages or one of many means by which white male civility is established and held in place. Nothing in this process accounts for antiblack violence and what such acts might make of white male civility or how such a legacy of ongoing aggression might mar that position, making it sustainable only through specific forms of domination and destruction. Every animal in the scenario Lundblad invokes is either property or available to death at a human being's hands. This is what gives weight to the mercy of the humane individual, the notion that all life *is in a position to be spared*, indeed that being in relation to another entity and not enacting violence on it is to be noted as a mark of exceptional character.

Though such logic is predicated on a set of untenable claims, it is nonetheless at play, not as an object of mockery but as a dominant discourse to be contended with, in *Native Son*'s opening scene. Before readers can contend with the way Bigger approaches animal life or that of his own kin, they have to first consider the substandard living conditions that Bigger and his family live through each day. Setting the scenes in such order creates a very different image of the relationship between dehumanization and the treatment of animals than what is presented by the discourse of humaneness. The economic oppression of black women and children is our port of entry into *Native Son* and serves as the condition of possibility for Bigger's initial act of violence. Before there is a dead black rat's body, there is a cramped kitchenette. Before there is the inhumane treatment of any animal, there is the inhumane set of circumstances that the characters set before us have been born into, an antiblack world that depends on a lack of empathy toward the black urban poor. In *12 Million Black Voices*, Wright argues,

> The kitchenette fills our black boys with longing and restlessness, urging them to run off from home, to join together with other restless black boys in gangs, that brutal form of city courage. The kitchenette piles up mountains of profits for the Bosses of the Buildings and makes them ever more determined to keep things the way they are. The kitchenette reaches out with fingers full of golden bribes to the officials of the city, persuading them to allow old firetraps to remain standing and occupied long after they should have been torn down. The kitchenette is the funnel through which our pulverized lives flow to ruin and death on city pavements, at a profit.[10]

Only a year after the publication of *Native Son*, Wright uses *12 Million Black Voices* to paint a vivid picture of the spaces in which black families were forced to live, whole "buildings which [were] dangerous for human habitation."[11] Thus, it is the substance of Bigger's domestic life that serves as its own argument against reductive claims about what borders mark the proper relationship between human and animal. For Wright, the matter of Bigger's rage and desperation is a sociological problem at root, more a result of his daily living conditions than any natural inclination toward cruelty. Wright chooses to render Bigger in a way that defies the bestialization of black boys and men not by invoking a kind of exceptionality in order to counter it, but by defamiliarizing the well-known tropes through which it functions. In the essay "Slouching toward Beastliness: Richard Wright's Anatomy of Thomas Dixon," Clare Eby writes,

> Wright interrogates the white fantasy about black "beasts" through a plot centering on a legal lynching in response to a presumed rape that in fact never occurred. Wright so closely examines Dixon's assumptions about black masculinity that *Native Son* needs to be seen as parodying the white supremacist vision. In anatomizing the "beast," Wright both follows and makes strategic revisions in the stereotype. Much as [Thomas] Dixon sought, by his own admission, to correct Stowe's influential representation of African-Americans, providing what he described as the "true story" of the South, . . . so did Wright seek to amend the consequential image of the black male "beast" and, with that, the portrait of the nation.[12]

Wright's primary investment is in a project of reclamation and revision, in sitting with the stereotype of the black male savage so that he might write life into it, imbuing it with a fullness that keeps readers from relinquishing their fear or setting it aside in the name of enjoyment. In sticking with an image so firmly ingrained into the public sphere, Wright forces his audience to wrestle with Bigger, the reader's own revulsion becoming a participant in the broader web of affect and influence that was of central concern to Wright when he crafted the text:

> Like Bigger himself, I felt a mental censor—product of the fears which a Negro feels from living in America—living in America—standing over me, draped in white, warning me not to write. This censor's warnings were translated into my own thought

process thus: "What will white people think if I draw the picture of such a Negro boy? Will they not at once say: 'See didn't
we tell you along that niggers are like that? Now, look, one of
their own kind has come along and drawn the picture for us!'" I
felt that if I drew the picture of Bigger truthfully, there would be
many reactionary whites who would try to make of him something I did not intend. And yet, and this was what made it difficult, I knew that I could not write of Bigger convincingly if I
did not depict him as he was: that is, resentful toward whites,
sullen, angry, ignorant, emotionally unstable, depressed and un-
accountable elated at times, and unable even, because of his own
lack of inner organization which American oppression has fos-
tered in him, to unite with members of his own race. . . . The
more I thought of it the more I became convinced that if I did
not write Bigger as I saw and felt him, if I did not try to make
him a living personality and at the same time a symbol of all the
larger things I felt and saw in him, I'd be reacting as Bigger
himself reacted: that is, I'd be acting out of fear if I let what
I thought whites would say constrict and paralyze me.[13]

Contra the sort of thinking that would seek to render Bigger as
savage or subhuman, Wright argues for a more expansive interpretation of his central character, one that repudiates white gaze
in favor of rendering black lives as those that are infinitely more
intricate than any humane/inhumane binary. His description of
Bigger's roots doubles as a refusal of a racialized pathology around
violent action and perceived emotional instability. The onus here
lies on the legalized forms of antiblackness that force black boys
and men to live under unabating pressure, a pressure that Wright
accounts for and emphasizes in his characterization of Bigger.

Wright revises the trope of the black male savage by giving us a character that lives into its most extreme claims while never releasing us from the confines of his personal war. This characterization of Bigger's emotional life as one that is not reducible to but is certainly influenced by his response to institutionalized racism and state surveillance is a staggering counterpunch to any argument in favor of Bigger's subpersonhood or irredeemable abjection.

Wright's unwillingness to play into a narrative of propriety or uplift exposes the myth of the savage for what it is, a way of reducing the lives of racial others who cannot bear the weight of fugitive possibility, of what happens when black authors opt out of writing explicitly against the grain of antiblack pathology and choose instead to revise it, to keep the painful tropes largely intact while remodeling their core elements. Bigger is more violent than he is kind, and that is precisely the point. He is in the world and of it. He is what the world has made him and exceedingly more. For Wright, there is no solace to be found in debating one's humanity. Instead, Wright embraces the pathological, allowing it to free him from the expectation of writing a brighter future. The bestialization of Bigger doubles as an argument for a more capacious black personhood, one that allows for something like evil or what evil makes possible.[14] The blackness that Richard Wright imagines has enough room for Bigger and whatever his opposite might be; it is the kind of empty that holds everything he needs.

❧

Of critical importance here are the ways in which Bigger is dehumanized not only through antiblack logics that would seek to construct him as inhumane or savage but also by environmental conditions that blur his relationship to the rat of the opening scene altogether and ultimately render him symbolically not as the savage destroyer of animal life but as the very animal life in question, as the pest that the exterminating forces in the book seek to uncover and destroy. In the essay "Invented by Horror: The Gothic and African American Literary Ideology in *Native Son*," James Smethurst writes,

> Perhaps the most telling moment of *Native Son* is the book's opening. First, an alarm clock goes off. The alarm clock ostensibly is a reminder of linear time. But in fact the alarm clock is a symbol of cyclical time marking the beginning of a day, a journey that will be almost exactly like yesterday and tomorrow. Immediately after the bell goes off, we are introduced to themes of confinement and transgressive sexuality. This transgressive sexuality is present explicitly in the shame that Bigger and his family feel about having to dress and undress in such close quarters. . . . Then a black rat appears, both terrified and terrifying. In the first moment of doubling in the text, Bigger kills his rat double, who attacks Bigger in a fit of terror, hunger, and defiance. Bigger goes on to terrify his sister with the dead rat, enjoying her fear. Bigger's mother prophesies a tragic end for him. End of story. But not really. There will be more rats. The slum buildings of the ghetto produce an endless stream of hungry and fearful rats. Bigger and his mother foresee Bigger's ending even if they don't grasp why such an ending is inevitable. But there will be more Biggers.[15]

Smethurst's reading of Bigger's inextricability from the rat of the opening scene is interesting primarily for what it obscures. Though Smethurst rightly picks up on the blackness of the rat as an initial clue of its metonymic ties to Bigger—he does not draw out or expand on this point, but his choice to gesture toward the rat's color, that is, "then a black rat appears, both terrified and terrifying," is important—there is, traveling along this vector of color and feeling, this darkness and terror that inhabit the same, small body, a strange conflation of blackness and the supposed *bleakness* of black social life. Reading the alarm clock as a sign that little in Bigger's life ever changes, indeed that the black quotidian is so devoid of energy that neither Bigger nor his family members experience each day anew, runs contrary to the narrative trajectory of, and external dialogues between, the characters themselves.[16]

What we see instead is a text full of characters that daily strive to make their lives anew, though those efforts are met with resistance on all sides. To understand Bigger's relationship to the rat as one that is purely reflective of their shared fear and hunger, and to mark either of those states as purely negative, is to ignore the myriad possibilities that linking Bigger's emotional life with that of the rat opens up. Though the rat in this scene can certainly be read as terrified, there is just as much evidence in the passage for a reading of the rat as an insurgent, as a stranger in Bigger Thomas's home that refuses to leave or live out its days on the periphery of the kitchenette. Instead, the rat interrupts the flow of daily life for the family. Its behavior is certainly marked by defiance, which Smethurst admits, but it should also be noted that what Smethurst reads as defiance, or even terror, is also a product of the rat being in the world, irrespective of intention. It is the mere presence of the rat that produces terror for everyone else in the apartment. It is the fact of its living, and the supposed threat of sickness or pain that its living imposes, that produces the rat as an object of fear and hatred, a creature that can be killed with impunity. In the swift move toward such negative doubling—one made feasible, we are left to imagine, by the utter abjection of black life in "the ghetto"—Smethurst fails to account for the generative possibilities of the zoomorphism he uncovers and thus misses out on what the figure of the rat produces, even in death, as Bigger's doppelganger.[17] If Smethurst is correct in his assertion that "there will be more rats, . . . there will be more Biggers," then the rat is no longer simply a site of trepidation, and longing, but rather immortality.[18]

For Smethurst, the rat is invulnerable. Though such a dynamic seems to depend on an interchangeability and fungibility of black lives that is altogether problematic—Smethurst's reading of Bigger's reproducibility is legibly bound up with an erasure of particularity or individual experience—such a reading nonetheless lends itself to a vision of an unkillable collective, a mass that rises up even and especially when one of its number is slain. Such tenacity, such hunger over and against the material conditions of a subjugation that doubles as the rats' condition of possibility, helps us to reimagine the interminable flow of rats in Smethurst's imagination as figures of resistance rather than solely of abjection or despair. Bigger's doubling renders him both killer and deceased, a move that produces a wide array of meanings that lead us much closer not only to the image of Bigger that Wright gestures toward in "How Bigger Was Born" but also to one that strains against such a pathological reading of both the world that produced Bigger and the one that currently produces what Smethurst would ostensibly read as Bigger's descendants, the "endless stream of hungry, fearful" black boys who dodge death as daily labor. Such totalizing pessimism is avoidable given a more generous reading of the text itself; what Smethurst interprets as apocalyptic prophecy from Bigger's mother could just as easily be seen as loving admonition:

"Suppose you wake up some morning and find your sister dead? What would you think then?" she asked. "Suppose those rats cut our veins at night when we sleep? Naw! Nothing like that ever bothers you! All you care about is your own pleasure! Even when the relief offers you a job you won't take it till they threaten to cut off your food and starve you! Bigger, honest you the most no-countest man I ever seen in all my life!"

"You done told me that a thousand times," he said, not looking round.

"Well, I'm telling you agin! And mark my word, some of these days you going to set down and cry. Some of these days you going to wish you had made something out of yourself, instead of just a tramp. But it'll be too late then."[19]

Later on in the dialogue, Bigger's mother continues: "'You'll regret how you living some day,' she went on. 'If you don't stop running with that gang of yours and do right you'll end up where you never thought you would. You think I don't know what you boys is doing, but I do. And the gallows is at the end of the road you travelling, boy. Just remember that.' She turned and looked at Buddy. 'Throw that box outside. Buddy.'"[20] This is certainly prophecy, but not necessarily in the way that Smethurst appears to think. Though there is a kind of prophetic forth-telling here, a naming of a present and problematic truth, this need not be interpreted solely or at all as a straightforward, *foretelling* prophecy that condemns Bigger, without mercy or hesitation, to an actual death. Such cruelty would be out of sync with Wright's characterization of Bigger's mother to this point. This is a moment of intense worry and fear for her, a fear articulated through reference to the danger presented by the threat of rats but one that is ultimately less about vermin as such and more about what makes their very presence, and the havoc they wreak on the family household, possible. For Bigger's mother, the rats are a reflection of Bigger's unwillingness to work, their boldness the product of Bigger's refusal to fulfill his role as eldest son, as a patriarchal figure of authority in the absence of a father whom Wright never sees fit to name. The extravagance of the gallows imagery that Bigger's mother employs is less about damning her son and more about her desire to save him, to set him right and see him live a fuller life, one detached from the deathly life he invests in, to his mother's mind, by spending time with his current cohort of friends. When Bigger tells his mother, "Stop prophesying about me," it is has little to do with his fear of a looming death that she has unique knowledge of and more to do with the weight of her disappointment, the pain that necessarily attends such hurtful words from a parent.[21]

This web of feeling is left unattended in Smethurst's analysis in favor of a one-to-one correlation between Bigger and the rats that populate his home, one that misses the richness of the exchanges in this portion of the text. The rat's grisly death is not merely a clue as to what comes later; it is a means through which the reader is more firmly grounded in the present and made aware of the individual relationships that have helped create the protagonist we will follow through the text. We are granted greater insight into Bigger's relationship to both Vera and his mother in this initial scene, and it is only through such insight that we can better understand any number of other ways that the figure of the rat is operating throughout the text as a whole. In *The Escape Motif in the American Novel: Mark Twain to Richard Wright*, Sam Bluefarb writes,

The opening scene of the novel is set in an urban tenement—a setting that could hardly be more appropriate for an act of escape—as distinct from those bucolic and semibucolic landscapes where most of the escapes dealt with in this study have taken place. This is the scene where the rat—that repulsive symbol of daily (and nightly!) life in the black ghetto—appears. The rat itself almost arouses our *sympathy*, as Bigger, who attempts to trap and kill him, will later arouse a similar compassion. However, the rat, as despicable as he is, is still a living thing. As such, if he merits revulsion, he also merits compassion; for not unexpectedly, both Bigger and the rat are (in the naturalistic mode) "victims of circumstance," inheritors of a "world they never made," blind creatures, threshing against an inscrutable force that would destroy them both, a world they would happily escape from given the opportunity. Of course, the rat of Book I will become Bigger himself. For like that rat, he too is trapped, in the first and in the last instance. Trapped as he is, however, he will try to escape his predetermined fate; and like the rat, he too will be destroyed by a frightened, uncomprehending (white) world.[22]

As is the case with Smethurst, Bluefarb's reading of the rat as Bigger's double fails to extend beyond the realm of the apocalyptic—in this case extending, explicitly, into the realm of the sympathetic—and in the process ignores a host of other possibilities made available by the novel's opening passage as it relates to the sort of symbolic work that the relationship between Bigger and the rat takes on. Bluefarb's analysis leaves our protagonist with too little wiggle room, spatially or otherwise, and opts instead for a rendering of Bigger's life as one fundamentally devoid of a certain dignity or freedom. According to this logic, Bigger is like the rat primarily in that his life is a cipher. As deployed here, the term "trapped" seems to connote the same kind of hopelessness that is all too common as far as contemporary interpretations of Bigger's inner life are concerned. Such a move often relies on a depiction of black social life broadly construed that evacuates all potential for flourishing due to material conditions, a logic by which the "ghetto" that both Smethurst and Bluefarb invoke comes to serve as a zone of no return, a space in which nothing grows or grieves. To think of Bigger and the rat as akin to each other in the sense that Bluefarb does, that is, as powerless victims held under the weight of an invisible sovereign, is to animalize Bigger in a way that forgoes other, more interesting approaches to the text. Neither Bigger nor the rat is a "blind, threshing" creature in the way that Bluefarb lays out here.[23] Lest we forget, the opening scene is not one of total domination or swift defeat but an extensive back-and-forth between Bigger and the invasive pest, a conflict in which Bigger eventually emerges victorious. Bigger is actually set on the defensive at the very beginning, when he is forced to contend with the rat's firm grip on his pant leg, the moment itself a reflection of its refusal to remain hidden or die in the shadows of the too-small room. The initial conflict between the rat and Bigger is an occasion that destabilizes Bluefarb's refusal to acknowledge Bigger's own refusal to be caged or killed for the majority of the novel:

> After Bigger takes the plunge into violence, Chicago's South Side becomes for him a labyrinth—Wright's word—from which there is no egress. Almost before he makes his first bid for freedom, he knows, more instinctively than rationally, that there is no true or lasting escape for him. Like the rat in the book's first pages, Bigger is trapped—except that he is no rat but a human being

caught in the grip of circumstances in a world he might have shared were life ordered in some other, more equitable way. . . . "He could not leave Chicago; all roads were blocked, and all trains, buses and autos were being stopped and searched. He was trapped. He would have to get out of this building. But where would he go?" Trapped. There is an irony here, since even the more familiar and innocuous amusement park labyrinth (or maze) has a way out, as well as a way in, assuming that one does not panic and disorient himself in the process of finding it. In Bigger's instance, the "escape" itself finally ends by becoming Bigger's greatest trap. Indeed—and it is doubtful how consciously aware Bigger is of this—if he would escape from the labyrinth of the city and society, he must first escape from the labyrinth of his own mind.[24]

Bluefarb's repeated emphasis on Bigger's lack of rationality and overreliance on instinct works to redouble the protagonist's animalization in a way that leaves him, rather fittingly, no way out. Not only is Bigger hemmed in on all sides, but he also, following this line of argument, lacks the reasoning capacity needed to fight back in any way that might make a dent. Both Bigger and the rat are largely hollow vessels in this sense, pure rage and hunger along a given vector. Such a misreading of Bigger's robust interior life, the contours of which the reader is made privy to at various points in the novel via the voice of an omniscient narrator, is baffling.

Though the acts of violence that Bigger commits throughout the novel certainly beg a number of questions about his empathy or willingness to exercise mercy in a given scenario, that Bigger remains a singularly thoughtful character throughout the text is difficult to deny. From his initial scheme to hide and eventually dispose of Mary Dalton's body to the later decisions that help him evade capture by police for the majority of the novel—to say nothing of his daily ruminations on his own place within the social field—the insight that Wright's narrator provides into Bigger's everyday thoughts are more than enough to challenge a reading of Bigger as an irrational actor. To obscure his intellectual labor in the service of a version of Bigger that marks all of his escape acts as futile products of instinct, and his very being as rooted in separation from the social world, does an injustice to a character that is plotting his next escape at every turn, if not through a new job or running from the police, then through dreams of another kind of flight altogether.[25] Such a reading also elides the rat's rich history in the US cultural imaginary as infinitely more than just a figure under duress, more than that which is always already condemned to a life of unending want. As Jonathan Burt's book-length ode to the animal in question, the aptly titled *Rat*, elucidates, the rat has historically been a site not only of lack but of seemingly infinite transgressive potential:

> Because the rat is an object of defilement and because notions of defilement and dirt are very much bound up with key symbolic boundaries of clean and unclean crucial to a general sense of order, then the rat logically should take its place on the far side of a border separating it from clean or the good. But, the symbolic order as much as the physical order is frail and can be easily threatened, especially around dangerous ideas that are so often associated with the horror of the rat: unbounded sexual reproduction, a limitless appetite, and dirt. Cultural attitudes to the rat reveal that it is a pollutant with the ability to move between bodily and symbolic boundaries with an overall trajectory that

seems to make it an especially threatening phenomenon as much in the realm of language and thought as in the granary or the food store. Like other dangerous objects, the rat constantly pushes at the edges of the borders set to contain it. Just to make matters worse, it also embodies a certain ambivalence. The rat is difficult to encode as a straightforwardly loathsome object partly because a refrain common in much writing on rats is that these creatures also inspire a sneaking, if sometimes sullen, admiration. The lascivious, greedy and cannibalistic rat, a stalwart harbourer of a good swatch of the Seven Deadly Sins, is also extremely smart, adaptable and even, for some writers, beautiful. And despite the rat's residence in ditches or sewers, it manages to stay remarkably clean and "preserves itself from pollution."[26]

The rat, according to Burt, is a figure full of contradiction, a fleet-footed signifier unwilling to stay still long enough to be held down or hemmed in by the limits of human expectation. As presented here, the rat is an ideal example of the ways in which actual, living animals explode the reductive significations that are so frequently mapped onto their bodies and in the process force the critic to recalibrate classic approaches to thinking something like ratness in a contemporary context. The opening scene of *Native Son* is perhaps a fitting place to begin such theorization. Taking up Burt's rigorous, graceful account avails a reading of Bigger-as-rat that is not easily conflated with a reading of the rat as solely a marker of death or bare life.[27] Burt's gesture toward the rat's numerous other symbolic functions primarily focuses instead on human misconception, on a widespread social fear of the rat predicated on unwarranted worries about its reproductive capacity and biological predisposition toward filth. Burt effectively argues that this is an archetype of the rat that is particularly difficult to shake: that of a creature that haunts every crevice and crack of the modern city, lying in wait to strike or strain the lack of resources in a given space. Yet such stereotypes also bleed into more interesting ways of thinking about the rat's movement not as an instinctual fleeing or penchant for theft but, to use Burt's terms, as a kind of adaptability. Put differently, in the animal kingdom, there are few escape artists on par with our rodent friends and fewer still that inspire such a wide array of responses from the dominant species.

The relationship between such effects / affects and a certain vision of blackness is much more complicated than what we see from Smethurst and Bluefarb. Instead of an affective economy in which blackness is solely a site of lack or nothingness, what we end up with instead is a vision of blackness—which is not only the blackness of the rat or the blackness of Bigger but also the blackness of the characters that populate the book and give it its full, unforgettable force—that, through the figure of the rat, is also linked to a persistence that is restorative. Bigger takes flight not out of what certain critics would have us think of as base instinct but for the love of freedom and the refutation of a social world in which he was trapped from the very beginning, marked since the day he was born. Bigger's adaptability fuels such flight and makes his prolonged evasion of arrest possible:

> He saw one of the men rise and flash a light. The circling beams lit the roof to a daylight brightness and he could see that one man held a gun. He would have to cross to other roofs before this man or others came upon him. They were suspicious and would comb every inch of space on top of these houses. On all fours, he scrambled to the next ledge and then turned and looked back; the

man was still standing, throwing the spot of yellow about over
the snow. Bigger grabbed the icy ledge, hoisted himself flat upon
it, and slid over. He did not think now of how much strength
was receded to climb and run; the fear of capture made him forget
even the cold, forget even that he had no strength left. From
somewhere in him, out of the depths of flesh and blood and bone,
he called up the energy to run and dodge with but one impulse:
he had to elude these men. He was crawling to the other ledge,
over the snow, on his hands and knees, when he heard the men
yell, "There he is!" The three words made him stop; he had been
listening for them all night and when they came he seemed to
feel the sky crashing soundlessly about hm. What was the use of
running? Would it not be better to stop, stand up, and lift his
hands high above his head in surrender? Hell, naw! He continued
to crawl.[28]

One imagines that it is just this kind of kinesthetic brilliance under
pressure that allows Bigger to survive the period before the book
begins, the narrative we are not granted access to which constitutes a kind of blankness before the chaos. Bigger's "hell, naw"
reads as a mantra here, the demurral of white civil society's control bodied forth in a moment of literal conflict with the state apparatus. In a moment when surrender would be the logical choice
for many people, Bigger opts into a different set of protocols altogether, choosing instead to seek egress, though the world may be
crashing all around him. This climactic scene of the book's second
movement, "Flight"—part of a broader triptych that composes the
text in its entirety: "Fear," "Flight," and "Fate"—is one that characterizes this section of the text as a whole and also gives new life
to the rat scene that opens "Fear," offering fresh insight into what

the slippage of Bigger Thomas and the black rat from the kitchenette might produce. Bigger's ability to process quickly in the midst of such sensory overload (the falling snow, the policemen shouting, the yellow lights dancing against the roof) reflects an adaptability that we see modeled elsewhere in the text, though not in such dramatic fashion. Here, we have Bigger "on all fours" crawling across the roof, fleeing from the force of the law, spinning the moment's fear into improvisatory genius.

Bigger is the rat in its most robust form here, its adeptness at escape and survival bodied forth in each dexterous maneuver, his hands against the ledge against the air. This is what so many readings of the opening scene (and thus also the later instances of pestiferous tenacity throughout the text) miss. It is a profound misunderstanding of both the nature of blackness and the nature of the history and biology of rats as a species that leads one to a deficit interpretation of our first encounter with Bigger and the kitchenette that gave birth to his ongoing refusal to be confined. Both Bigger and the rat are "dangerous objects," forms of insurgent life that refuse the limitations imposed from outside. To read Bigger's metaphorical ratness, which is irreducible to but nonetheless tied up with the rat's literal *and* figurative blackness—read: blackness as a site of denigration or availability to death—as pure lack is to ignore a body of zoological and historical data that unmakes such thinking, exposes it as unfounded myth in service of a history that never happened:

> The rat is, as some writers have phrased it, a twin of the human, and their mutual history is dark. In fact, the rat has been represented as the very debasement of evolution. If one devolves "downwards" from the human, one comes not to the ape or

monkey but to the rat. . . . In 1923 H. P. Lovecraft wrote a horror story entitled "The Rats in the Walls." In Lovecraft's comments on it he dwells on the topics of nature and evolution, and discusses the thesis that there were two separate lines of racial development, in his terminology Caucasian and Negro. These derived from different types of ape but at root they shared a common ancestry of extreme bestiality. "Certain traits in many lower animals suggest, to my mind whose imagination is not dulled by scientific literalism, the beginnings of activities horrible to contemplate in evolved mankind." "The Rats in the Walls" is a story, among other things, of such a descent through layers of cultural and natural evolution to the most primeval, base, and horrific level of human activity. What we reach at the bottom of this descent, however, is not the basest of human simian ancestry, but the rat.[29]

What emerges from the midst of this shared relegation to theory's underground, far from the inimitable glow of reason? Such subterranean living produces something other than emptiness, nothing less than an unbounded plenitude set free from the gaze of those who dwell above ground. In the rooftop scene from "Flight," we encounter Bigger as a character of singular improvisatory talent, one straining against a system predicated on the notion that he, the humanoid pest in flight, creeps and crawls at the nadir of the social ladder, leeching resources from those above.

From the very beginning, we see Bigger fleeing, fleeing always because *that* is the central argument of the primal scene—not that Bigger and his family are beyond repair, or at all broken, but that survival is flight by another name. Bigger is not fleeing from the police alone but, as is the case in Burt's extensive study of the rat, from an entire system of thought that would brand him as the un-making of the human project, a dark mark on the very subjec-tivity he should seek to attain. Bigger too lives on the margins of what many critics imagine as a full, human life and as such has been taken up in the popular imagination as that rare protagonist that doubles as an ultimate other, an archetypal criminal mind onto which we might project our greatest fears and anxieties. Yet neither Wright nor Burt permits such a straightforward take on their subjects of interest. "Flight" instead becomes the tale of an unkillable outlaw on the run, a central figure that dodges death at each corner while headed nowhere in particular. This striving toward nowhere is also the expression of the desire for an else-where, a place far away from the extended reach of the law. This desire is bodied forth emphatically in the "hell, naw" of the afore-mentioned passage, in the crawling and leaping and running that stand in composite as the choreography of his ongoing escape, his refusal of the "there he is" uttered by the policemen on his tail.[30]

It is Bigger's transgression of the law that blackens him beyond what can be allowed to let live or linger, the violence he enacts against Mary Dalton that renders him the object of vermin con-trol. Bigger's understanding of this shift in his position is his cen-tral motivation for fleeing from home, an escape that operates in most profound contradistinction to widely accepted readings of the text as one that is marked primarily by a certain orientation toward death and the ever-looming threat of its swift approach. Even out-side of critics like Smethurst of Bluefarb, contemporary theorists too often ascribe an utter lack of possibility to the opening scene of *Native Son* that forecloses the reading practice that serves as the core of this study. Put differently, such texts offer readings that do not necessarily account for the fugitivity that is immanent to these figures, even and especially when they are under extreme duress.

There is a persistence that these writers cannot deny, even as they obscure it within an entangling pathology that leaves little room for beauty or breath. The difficulty of moving away from such a reading is exemplified in Abdul R. JanMohamed's brilliant study *The Death-Bound-Subject: Richard Wright's Archaeology of Death*, in which he deftly moves, within the space of mere pages, between a reading of the rat scene that traffics in much of the thanatocentric language that characterizes aforementioned earlier critics of Wright and what reads as a much more capacious interpretation of Bigger's relationship to the figure of the animal and what such a relation means for how we are to read the role of the pest in the text's opening scenes:

> The rich symbolism and ambiguity of the famous rat scene that opens the novel allow it to be interpreted in diverse ways. However, from the perspective of the dialectic of death that preoccupies Wright, the scene's primary function is to map the zone of bare life as one fundamental border that defines Bigger's subjectivity. . . . Here Wright emphasizes the disruption, by the rat, of the precarious, ritualized civility on which is predicated the humanity of the four people in the room. The four people (Bigger's two siblings and his mother) living in this one-room kitchenette in absolute poverty and lack of any privacy manage to maintain their human dignity via a ritual in which the boys dress first while the women turn their backs, and vice versa. By provoking panic and chaos, the rat's entrance disrupts the minimal human dignity afforded by this form of civility and

threatens to banish entirely the routine ceremony that establishes their humanity. Bigger's subsequent crushing of the rat, its
"actual-death," permits the humans to return to the ritual that
defines their minimal humanity. Throughout the novel, Bigger
repeatedly uses the term *blotting out* to characterize his desire to
kill various human beings who are perceived as penetrating into
his "bare life," the zone within which his social death permits him
to "live."[31]

JanMohamed's emphasis on the precarious, unwieldy nature of
Bigger's everyday life—even to the point that he places the word
"live" in quotation marks at the very end of this particular passage—
marks his reading of the novel's opening as one that necessarily
decenters the potential, if not for resistance, then at least for the
presence and persistence of everyday living, an ordinariness that
is undoubtedly something other than social death or bare life but
might be better described as a third space between utter despair
and the various markers of wealth or wellness that would legibly
distance Bigger's family from the kind of abjection that so many
interlocutors of Wright have read into the text.[32] Yet just as quickly
as JanMohamed presents the reader with what seems like more of
the same—though it is worth mentioning that his work's invocation of Orlando Patterson provides a theoretical framework for
thinking Bigger's life as death that is arguably more compelling
than much of what precedes it—he pivots the reader away from
a deficit reading and into a (re)vision of animality that leaves
space for alternative, otherworldly possibility. JanMohamed writes,
"Bigger's future is symbolized by the rat, which, in the face of its
condemnation to death, resists the inevitable with tenacity and

defiance. By constructing these . . . horizons or borders of death, Wright prefigures Bigger's 'fate.' . . . The recognition (and the embracing) of death . . . eventually becomes the precondition of his freedom."[33] When imagined as a figure of defiance, as the embodiment of insurgent life over and against the systemic deployment of death that rarely relents and is ever shifting in its protocols and forms, the rat avails itself to the contemporary reader as a kind of trap door, a way outside the text's well-received logic of ubiquitous sorrow and decay. Wright's rat is familiar with the imminence of death, how large it looms. Nonetheless, in this interpretation of events, that the rat is eventually going to die *is altogether beside the point*. JanMohamed's gesture toward the rat's pluck, its foolish refusal, creates fertile ground for a consideration of what strains in and through and against the social death he names and so meticulously outlines, of how black folks survive even when they are outcast and outgunned and outlawed and outstripped, how they nonetheless go about living through the everyday.

Ultimately, the bridge that Wright builds, and that Jan-Mohamed shores up, between Bigger's daily struggle and the world of the rat is not a gesture of dehumanization but rather fresh insight into the universal particularity of such blackness, an outsiderness that flourishes in the shadow of white civil society and its (anti)social field. Both Bigger and the rat are able to live outside the "epistemology of ignorance" that Charles Mills describes as an undercurrent of daily social life for white signatories of the Racial Contract.[34] These figures represent a disruptive social force that knows no outside order and needs none in order to function. In lieu of "the good life," both Wright's rat and his protagonist choose worlds that exist only inside the walls and under the floorboards, the myriad lives made possible by the cover of darkness and dirt.[35]

❀

The 4,000 or so haiku that Richard Wright penned toward the end of his life articulate an account of his relationship to the figure of the pest, and animal life broadly construed, that is altogether different from what appears in much of his other work.[36] The 817 spare, difficult poems that constitute his final book, *Haiku: This Other World*, were, according to Wright's daughter Julia, who penned the text's introduction, in some ways the textual embodiment of Wright's own health troubles toward the end of his life. To her mind, the haiku served as "self-developed antidotes against illness."[37] Such an understanding of Wright's process, as well as the material conditions in which he produced his final work—that is, he wrote all of these poems while ailing from amoebic dysentery and living in Parisian exile—is productive for a contemporary return to what this work might mean when considered as part of a larger tradition of black writers articulating their relationship to the ever-looming threat of death—physical, psychic, social, civic, or otherwise—through the figure of the animal.

Although there are certainly any number of animal figures that populate Wright's haiku—dogs, crows, cats, and cows are repeat offenders—I want to concentrate here on what the rats are up to. Wright's haiku have received a fair amount of critical attention over the past ten years, but there has been little extensive focus on the specific doings of the animal figures in these poems, as most scholarship on this work has tended in the direction of reading his haiku as a form of nature writing in a broad sense, without much focus on the animals themselves or what such a relationship between a

black writer and animal life might mean as part of a larger trend
in post-Emancipation-era black literatures.[38]

Thus, my primary aim here is to home in on several of Wright's
haiku, in particular, numbers 74, 21, 114, and 795, as a means
through which to finally set foot on heretofore-untraveled roads
that Wright maps out for us, largely by refusing to temper the pre-
occupation with rats that can be found all throughout his corpus.
We have already seen from Wright's placement of Bigger Thomas
vis-à-vis the figure of the rat that Wright is hip to its potential as
a symbol of escape. Here, we are granted access to a separate component of the rat's affective arsenal: its capacity to hide, to haunt.
If we can agree with Wright's assessment of the work, his claim
that "these poems are the result of [his] being in bed a great deal
and it is likely that they are bad," then I wonder what sort of beauty
might bloom from this badness or lack of vigor, what approach to
rendering the rat spills forth from so much time spent lying still,
dreaming of the other locales that the rat's size and swiftness make
available, if only through the reach that metaphor provides.[39]

Haiku 21 is a notable example of Wright's deployment of rats
as figures of haunting, in part because no rat actually appears
within the body of the poem itself:

> On winter mornings
> The candle shows faint markings
> Of the teeth of rats.[40]

In this selection, the rat's presence, or perhaps even the presence
of many rats, a legion of rats untold and unthought, is signaled by
the very absence of any body whatsoever, by the trace the rat bodies
leave behind. That these etchings are left in candle wax, an instru-
ment that might be used to ward off pests with its heat and light,

is a testament to the resolve of these particular rats, their commitment to being seen. There is also a gesture here toward the insatiable hunger of pest animals in the city: these rats that were trying to eat a candle whole if not snuff out its glow. The rats in haiku 21 leave a calling card but never show their faces. They thieve in the night and clear out before day breaks their cover. The markings they leave function in part as a reflection of the condition and quality of the speaker's home. One assumes that a wealth of candles might imply the absence of electricity or heat. Early on, then, we have a sense of the class struggle that is built into these poems. These are not the haiku of a speaker enmeshed in nature, free from the trappings of domestic life. These are works directly engaged with the forms of animal life that the poor are forced to grapple with every day, the natural objects that refuse to remain in nature and dare to dwell where they are not wanted.

Haiku 74 clues us into yet another instance in which rats are deployed as such hidden, liminal figures. Unlike their kin in haiku 21, the rats in question here leave no physical evidence whatsoever of their nightly activities, only the phonic matter of their movement:

> The sound of a rat
> Scampering over cold tin
> Is heard in the bowels.[41]

The open-endedness of the poem's last line generates an impasse here. By stanza's end, the reader cannot be sure of where the rat is exactly. If the "bowels" that Wright refers to here are indeed the bowels of the speaker's home at the moment of writing, the apartment that appears in so many of the haiku in *This Other World*, then what are we to make of the doubleness of the term, the hunger it gestures toward, the way it serves to anthropomorphize the apartment. With an approach that differs greatly from the one deployed in haiku 21, Wright produces a sense of trepidation in the reader not through the visually perceptible clue—droppings on the window sill or teeth marks on the candles or holes in a loaf of bread—but through the very sound of rats moving. The scampering rats of haiku 74 are fully present. They are with us in the moment of reading. They are close enough that we can hear their footsteps but far enough that the speaker can register a great distance between their body and his body, between the underground of the apartment's inner walls, its bowels, and its primary stage, the desk from which he writes. Notice too the distance of the passive voice, "the sound of a rat . . . is heard," which rings differently, of course, than *I hear the sound of rats*. While assigning the hearing of the rats' footsteps to a single figure might have given life to a reading of this poem as a reflection on a frightening, individual experience, what Wright's use of the passive voice allows for is an image of the apartment as overrun with the sound of claws, of countless rats scraping against the cold tin of what holds the very structure of the speaker's home in place. The sound of rats is heard by anyone in earshot of their collective movement, anyone forced to be still and suffer their distant music. A similar theme permeates one of Wright's later haiku, number 114, which shares an opening line with number 74, though it pivots in a slightly different direction one line later:

> The sound of a rat
> Gnawing in the winter wall
> Of a rented room.[42]

The direct action of haiku 114 moves in stark contrast to that of the aforementioned haiku in which rats are central actors. Whereas haiku 21 offers little more than teeth markings to indicate the rat's presence and haiku 74 eschews such visual evidence altogether, opting instead to linger in the fear generated by the sounds of countless tiny feet moving through the depths of the speaker's home, the rat that serves as the subject of haiku 114 gets right to the business of consumption. Whether the animal is gnawing on food from within the walls of the apartment or gnawing on the walls themselves is altogether unclear. What is undeniable is the voracious hunger of the rat that is made palpable in the second and third lines. Wright's choice of "gnawing" lends a sense of temporality to the description of the scene, setting up what feels like the inevitable breakthrough of this rat and untold others beyond the border of the walls and into the room itself, a break that would eradicate any and all boundaries between speaker and object, between the proper occupant of the room and the interloper we know only by the noise of its desire. The rented room we are introduced to here has a similar feel to the setting of both haikus 21 and 74. These are spaces we know only by what is not supposed to be there, by the surplus noise and jagged etchings left behind by vermin that eat and move and destroy with relative impunity. A far cry from any form of haiku that might "express the poet's union with nature," what we find in these works from Wright are strong gestures toward the various kinds of conflict and fissure that emerge from sharing space with unexpected visitors that have no intention of leaving.[43] These are poems motivated by a generative *disunity*, an extended acknowledgment of the peculiar ecology of affects that pest animals produce. There is no indication that the speaker is especially fond of these rats or even that he carries a certain ambivalence regarding whether they remain or not. The predominant emotion undergirding these poems is a sense of de-

tached awe, a willingness to engage with the singular power that
rats hold in such a cramped space. Wright paints a robust picture
of what it might mean to participate in an ecosystem in which
human dominance is completely destabilized by spatial restriction.
There is little uncertainty as to which party feels most at ease in
these poems. Wright is not the master of this domain. Such control belongs primarily to the rats that populate these poems and
serve as their principal object of interest:

> However much we may seek to extrapolate the rat from its un-
> natural surroundings and view it as a "natural" creature with
> which the speaker in the haiku is somehow attuned, we cannot
> escape the image of the savage rat, trapped, wheeling, and at-
> tacking Bigger. Even if such an intertextual elision were pos-
> sible, the two haiku contain a sense of menace: the first results
> from the disconcerting noise of claws on tin, and the second from
> the rat attempting to chew its way through the wall and into the
> speaker's apartment. The point of view of the haiku is also inter-
> esting. Rather than using a subjective "I" to personalize the ex-
> periences, Wright suggests that they are universal; anyone who
> is impoverished could have the same experience.[44]

This passage, taken from Richard Iadonisi's "'I Am Nobody': The
Haiku of Richard Wright," is compelling largely because of its
focus on the agency of the animal figures at play. Iadonisi's claim
that there is a "sense of menace" to the rat's movements, as opposed
to raw hunger or the desire for safety, indexes the sort of unbound
possibility when it comes to animal behavior that Wright makes
space for in these haiku and beyond.[45] It is Wright's ongoing commitment to such capacity that leads to my primary point of contention with Iadonisi's reading of what constitutes the intersection

between the rat that attacks Bigger in the beginning of *Native Son* and the rats in Wright's haiku. Where Iadonisi sees "menace" and "savage" animals bent on inflicting harm, I imagine that Wright left room for us to see creatures committed to their own survival, ones whose everyday comings and goings are sources of fear only for those who live outside their sensory world. Though both the scampering feet in haiku 74 and the "gnawing" teeth in haiku 114 can be envisioned as attempts to undermine or unmake the lived environment of the speaker, they could just as easily register as banal activity, misrecognized and aligned by an unwitting observer, a speaker who knows well enough to fear the pest but understands little to nothing about its interior life. It is only in the last of the haiku in *This Other World*, number 795, that we get a glimpse into such interiority, albeit in a way that fits rather neatly into the accusations of anthropomorphism that Wright's haiku have faced since their publication:[46]

> A tolling church bell:
> A rat rears in the moonlight
> And stares at the steeple.[47]

One of the final haiku in the collection, number 795, serves as a compelling counter not only to Iadonisi's menacing, "savage" rats but also to any number of other depictions of rats that are prevalent throughout *This Other World*. In stark contrast to the rat that is forced to hide or haunt, one that can only leave its trace but never move freely in the open without the fear of death, we have here a rat that takes the time to contemplate, one that, rather fittingly given what we know about the author, stands alone that it might think and do so uninterrupted. This final rat is illegible as a pest animal in any meaningful sense. We do not know whether it lives outside or inside the apartment, whether it has stolen any food or takes up residence in the walls at night. All we are given is a set of physical gestures—its rearing and staring that are perhaps rooted in, but nonetheless exist in excess of, instinct or reflex. This is more than an animal reacting to the sound of potential danger. What Wright creates in this scene is a respite from the unrelenting danger of the domestic sphere, an open space in which the rat might dwell or imagine the world as if it were otherwise.

2

Cock

The survey says all groups can make more money
if they lose weight except black men ... men of other colors
and women of all colors have more gold, but black men
are the summary of weight, a lead thick thing on the scales,
meters spinning until they ring off the end of the numbering
of accumulation, how things grow heavy, fish on the
ends of lines that become whales, then prehistoric sea life
beyond all memories, the billion days of human hands
working, doing all the labor one can imagine

—Afaa Michael Weaver, "American Income"

The very essence of the male animal, from the bantam rooster
to the four-star general, is to strut. Indeed, in 19th century
America, a particular type of exaggerated male boastfulness became almost a national style. Not for the Negro male.

—Daniel Patrick Moynihan, "The Moynihan Report"

Hold fast to dreams
For if dreams die
Life is a broken-winged bird
That cannot fly.

—Langston Hughes, "Dreams"

How might we configure the limits and lacunae of the black masculine as a mode or means of thinking gender? What does it call into being or put under erasure the moment it arrives on the scene? What texts, both inside and outside the realm of literary criticism, are available to the contemporary reader interested in parsing out the ways in which black boys and men move through text at the level of representation and symbol, which is also to say, what lessons do we glean from the US American literary canon about *what black men are,* how they live, or whether their living is always already a spectacular kind of dying? Further, if one were to respond to such a claim or question of black male social life as a form of death in the negative, how might we theorize and historicize the ways in which death has come to serve as the dominant frame for thinking black male experience in the US and abroad?[1] For the purposes of this chapter, I am interested in working through and against discourses that imagine little else for black men beyond the grave and furthermore in gathering such materials to think toward a theory of the black masculine that shatters prevailing, pathological assumptions about what such lives can bear or bear forth and ultimately aims to build something fresh from the shards.

Toni Morrison's oeuvre is a singular resource for such an endeavor. There is already an extensive body of work on the ways in which her characters open up new worlds for thinking identity across lines of perceptible difference, alternate realities that avail to us more transgressive models for race, gender, and disability in particular.[2] Though much has been written about Morrison's work in this vein, few scholars have explored the role of nonhuman actors, and nonhuman animals in particular, in Morrison's ongoing argument against strict, bounded markers of identity that leave no room for growth or play. Such characters abound in Morrison's fiction—Here Boy, Sethe and Denver's dog in *Beloved*, the horses ridden by the tribe of blind warriors in *Tar Baby*, and the flock of birds that follows the titular character of *Sula* all come to mind—but rarely do such animal characters take center stage as a means through which a given character becomes an object of analysis. In one of Morrison's novels in particular, *Song of Solomon*, I will argue, Morrison's emphasis on the presence and, most importantly, the *properties* of animals is notably gendered and provides a fertile ground for imagining a theory of the black masculine grounded in literary analysis.

Put somewhat differently, I am interested in the ways in which Toni Morrison uses animals, and birds in particular, to make a certain argument about how it *feels* to be a black man, how she deploys them in order not only to critique the limiting, violent ways in which black masculinity is structured from the outside but also to describe the means through which black men and boys bear such weight, how they comport themselves under the duress of everyday life as a perceived threat. Following Afaa Weaver's suggestion that "black men are the summary of weight," I would like to track the way that black masculinity as heaviness, as excess, as adornment, as vanity, as *exorbitance* moves through *Song of Solomon* in the bodies of birds, how these animals, rather paradoxically, come to signal a certain boundedness to earth, an unwieldy abundance that limits all possibility of escape or futurity.[3] Alongside Nahum Chandler and others, however, I would like to think imaginatively about what such exorbitance avails to us as a frame for imagining alternative black masculinities and to begin with the premise of abundance rather than absence.[4] Using some of Morrison's most well-known characters—Milkman Dead; his best friend, Guitar;

and his father, Macon Dead II—as central examples, I will close read moments of interspecies interaction with birds in the text in an effort to elucidate the generous approach to thinking black masculinity, and black personhood in a broader sense, that Morrison's work provides.

By theorizing a Morrisonian vision of black masculinity as always already bound up with a certain heaviness, a haunting presence that doubles as a kind of beauty but also prevents something like flight or a legible form of social mobility, I intend both to contribute to an ongoing conversation around representations of black maleness and to trouble some of the arguments that have historically given coherence to that field. Following Morrison's lead, my aim is to make an argument for an unfamiliar, destabilizing constellation of masculinities, one that transcends and unmoors reductive ways of thinking the intersection of blackness and gender. Central to this argument will be an extended consideration of the social milieu into which Milkman Dead is thrown, a world that marks and mars him from birth as the carrier of numerous traits that differentiate him from other black men in the text. I am interested in exploring this distance, this discomfort, at the level of feeling and in examining what Milkman's experiences throughout *Song of Solomon* elucidate about the way real-world masculinities come to be formed and how they might be critically desedimented in the service of a fugitivity that might ease the weight of living while black and male and yet unburied, unfettered, unbowed.

❀

The opening scene of *Song of Solomon* betrays the novel's obsession with failed flights, its persistent concern with what happens when a body misapprehends its own, unbearable heaviness. The first example of such failure in the text is deeply ironic, even to the point of tragedy, largely because of its object, a salesman by the name of Robert Smith:

> The North Carolina Mutual Life Insurance agent promised to fly from Mercy to the other side of Lake Superior at three o'clock. Two days before the event was to take place he tacked a note on the door of his little yellow house:
>
> > At 3:00 p.m. on Wednesday the 18th of February, 1931, I will take off from Mercy and fly away on my own wings. Please forgive me. I loved you all.
> > (signed) Robert Smith,
> > Ins. Agent
>
> Mr. Smith didn't draw as big a crowd as Lindbergh had four years earlier—not more than forty or fifty people showed up—because it was already eleven o'clock in the morning, on the very Wednesday he had chosen for his flight, before anybody read the note. At that time of day, during the middle of the week, word-of-mouth news just lumbered along.[5]

My primary interest in this scene lies in what is underemphasized or altogether unsaid. First, there is the matter of Robert Smith's profession. That Smith, a man who is well versed in the manifold dangers of everyday life by virtue of his work as a life insurance agent—and who also, it is worth mentioning, has a small, yellow house that registers metonymically as a reflection of his own persistent caution or fear—would choose to engage in a public act of such exceptional risk is bizarre. This is not to say that one need work in life insurance to comprehend the dangers of jumping off a building, but the extremity of contrast is generative here, as it conveys, rather vividly, the depth of Smith's conviction. The note he leaves strengthens such a reading. Its ambiguous ending initially reads, perhaps, as a suicide note but also as a good-bye letter, and it is a reflection of the depth of thought that serves as prelude to his grand escape.

This is the second sort of jarring contrast we see at work in this primal scene: the clash between the morose, deeply personal nature of Smith's note, on the one hand, and the bombastic, rather colorful character of the act itself, on the other: an act that is publicized, ostensibly, for the sake of attendance and features unexpected flourishes, the most stark of which are the "blue silk wings" he dons in order to facilitate takeoff.[6] If Smith is going to fly, he will do so in style. Note also the contrast Morrison draws between Smith's declaration of his plans to fly and the slow, lumbering manner in which the news of his experiment travels. Dreams, the argument follows, take on a kind of weight when they are put into the world. To dream aloud is to invite critique or, worse perhaps, indifference. From the first scene, Morrison places this nexus before us: the conflict between a man's desire to fly, *his desire to be seen doing so,* and a social world that can opt in or out of bearing the burden of that spectacle. Smith's willingness to attempt this dangerous feat, one complicated by his aforementioned career choices, is inextricable from a certain refusal of invisibility, his silken wings, as well as the note he plasters to the front of his home, both operating as embodiments of his yearning for engagement, both objects working in different ways to ensure that his plan is successful both as a mode of egress and as a means of entertainment. An aesthete, Smith wants even his leaving to be beautiful.

Such flair or flash appears to be a rather recent development for Smith and is largely out of step with how he is characterized not too long after the text's opening scene:

> They kidded him, abused him, told their children to tell him they were out or sick or gone to Pittsburgh. But they held on to those little yellow cards as though they meant something—laid them gently in the shoe box along with the rent receipts, marriage licenses, and expired factory identification badges. Mr. Smith smiled through it all, managing to keep his eyes focused almost the whole time on his customers' feet. He wore a business suit for his work, but his house was no better than theirs. He never had a woman that any of them knew about and said nothing in church but an occasional "Amen." He never beat anybody up and he wasn't seen after dark, so they thought he was probably a nice man. But he was heavily associated with illness and death, neither of which was indistinguishable from the brown picture of the North Carolina Mutual Life Building in the back of their yellow cards. Jumping from the roof of Mercy was the most interesting thing he had done. None of them had suspected he had it in him. Just goes to show, they murmured to each other, you never really do know about people.[7]

What does it cost to be unknown or unloved? For Smith, such semianonymity was experienced alongside persistent abuse from his customers and fellow townspeople, an ire that is in some ways understandable given the regularity with which he asked them for money ("more regular than the reaper," according to one source).[8] This constant levying of funds, combined with Smith's relative quietude in other avenues of town social life—public romance, performances of exuberance in church, and so on—served to

create a rift between Smith and the rest of the social world, a
dehiscence that he sought to mend in this moment of audience
engagement, this final request. Over and against a reading that
might lead us to understand Smith's attempt at flight as the long-
awaited break of a repressed figure in search of release, Morrison's
robust characterization also leaves space for a vision of Robert
Smith as a man dedicated to certain forms of order and restraint,
one who did not break as much as he decided to break out, break
free. It is not life as such that Smith wants to escape but rather the
kind and caliber of life that is possible in the small Michigan town
he wishes to be rid of. The townspeople are, ultimately, correct.
One cannot "know about" another in any totalizing sense. Following Morrison's characterization of Smith as someone who
never did anything more "interesting" than jump from the roof of
Mercy Hospital, who never had a public relationship of any sort or
bothered anyone beyond what was required by his job, a flock of
critical questions rises to the fore.[9] Who or what convinced Smith
that he could fly in the first place? And, once such a conviction
had taken hold, what would this sort of a man feel the need to take
flight from? At the textual level, no tenable answer to the first
question appears. To the second question, however, his letter re-
plies, albeit in muted tones: the love that Robert Smith describes,
the love that is largely missing from the descriptions of Smith
given by the townspeople—that is, that he is either bewilderingly
dull or downright annoying—and can thus be described as an unrequited love, a love that pushed Smith to beg forgiveness not only
for his leaving but also for his dull, dogged affection. In this way,
Morrison provides the reader with an entrée into the affective
economy of the text, one that will feature a web of relations
marked by unreciprocated affection, by burden without release.

Robert Smith's desire to fly is in many ways singular as it pertains to the ensemble of black male characters in *Song of Solomon*. The exorbitance he strains against is not rooted in vanity, a desire for revenge, or commitment to the accrual of material possessions— to be sure, these vices are primary sources of frustration for almost every other male character in the novel—but rather in his banality, the boredom and outright indifference he inspires in his neighbors and clients. In a sense, this popular perception of Smith as a forgettable figure seems almost preordained. Morrison is renowned for her flair when it comes to naming characters.[10] What are we to make of a figure so plainly plumed, one that walks with a common name in a textual universe full of color? Consider the following passage from later in the novel, long after Smith's demise:

> He closed his eyes and thought of the black men in Shalimar, Roanoke, Petersburg, Newport News, Danville, in the Blood Bank, on Darling Street, in the pool halls, the barbershops. Their names. Names they got from yearnings, gestures, flaws, events, mistakes, weaknesses. Names that bore witness. Macon Dead, Sing Byrd, Crowell Byrd, Pilate, Reba, Hagar, Magdalene, First Corinthians, Milkman, Guitar, Railroad Tommy, Hospital Tommy, Empire State (he just stood around and swayed), Small Boy, Sweet, Circe, Moon, Nero, Humpty, Dumpty, Blue Boy, Scandinavia, Quack-Quack, Jericho, Spoonbread, Ice Man, Dough Belly, Rocky River, Gray Eye, Cock-a-Doodle-Doo, Cool Breeze, Muddy Waters, Pinetop, Jelly Roll, Fats, Lead Belly, Bo Diddley, Cat-Iron, Peg-Leg, Son, Shortstuff, Smoky Babe, Funny Papa, Bukka, Pink, Bull Moose, B.B., T-Bone, Black Ace, Lemon, Washboard, Gatemouth, Cleanhead, Tampa Red, Juke Boy, Shine, Staggerlee, Jim The Devil, Fuck-Up and *Dat* Nigger.[11]

What does the name Robert Smith bear witness to? What mistake or weakness, what flaw or yearning? If we are to read the preceding passage as a theory of naming for Morrison, then it becomes difficult not to see Robert Smith's very name as a gesture toward either blandness—that is, that Smith has never done anything that would make him worthy of a nickname—or a long-standing distance from the sorts of social spaces, and caring, playful relationships, that would serve as the condition of possibility for such naming, such proximity rendered in language. Both readings dovetail in a fashion that supports the earliest descriptions of Smith. This was a man of duty with little to distract him from it, not even the love he writes about in the note he leaves behind as a final farewell. Smith was loved without return and, in the process, disinvested in more than just the town and its capacity for a certain vision of social life but also, it would appear, in scientific law. He never frames his flight as anything other than just such an escape. All the reader is made privy to in the way of description is Smith's claim that the wings he will use as instruments of egress are "all his own."[12] Like so much else in his life, his wings are shared with no one.

Robert Smith's death looms large over the novel and serves as the connecting thread through which one can trace the critical role of animal presence, and animal symbolism, in *Song of Solomon*. Like so many of the characters that appear in the novel once his death becomes mere memory, Smith's very person was indelibly marked not only by his *inability to fly* but also by his steadfast desire to do so, even against conventional wisdom or scientific discourse. It is his yearning in the face of such facts, this exorbitant will over and against systemic boundaries that would ostensibly foreclose such dreams long before one could engage in the sort of behavior for which the townspeople most vividly remember him, that is of central concern. How does such yearning take hold? How do this novel's black men in particular—ones who live with constant reminders of their own limitations, physical, financial, and otherwise, and indeed the truth that their everyday lives are impinged upon by sociolegal restraints that function as persistent, undeniable limits—make up in their minds that this sort of *groundedness*, this exorbitant weight, is all they will ever know? It is in this sense, that is, as an event that opens a series of questions about how the novel's central, metonymic ensemble functions as a proxy for real-world experiences of antiblack violence, that Robert Smith's failed flight becomes an instructional moment not only for the reader but also for other characters in the text, none more so than Milkman Dead:

> The next day a colored baby was born inside Mercy for the first time. Mr. Smith's blue silk wings must have left their mark, because when the little boy discovered, at four, the same thing Mr. Smith had learned earlier, that only birds and airplanes could fly—he lost all interest in himself. To have to live without that single gift saddened him and left his imagination so bereft that he appeared dull even to the women who did not hate his mother. The ones who did, who accepted her invitations to tea and envied the doctor's big dark house of twelve rooms and the green sedan, called him "peculiar."[13]

This origin story—both that of Milkman Dead as the first black baby born inside Mercy (which, I think, Morrison intends as a kind of double entendre, a moment meant to index a geographical space of particular historical import within the narrative but also to have us consider the various forms of mercy that Milkman is shown throughout the text and how said mercy informs the way he comports himself) and that of Milkman's ongoing disappointment in the weight of his own body, that is, the unshakeable realization that he, not unlike Robert Smith, is built for pursuits other than flight—sets up the novel's central conflict.

First, the opening presents us with the question of what Milkman is to make of his own heaviness, how he is to manage a body that does not move the way he wants it to or is read in ways that run counter to his expectations and desires. Second, the reader is made privy here to the first time that Milkman must navigate the gaze of others, in particular, the women he encounters who find him to be "peculiar," a term that swings in its register between the negative and the affirmative throughout the text. Robert Smith, now dead as the name that sutures Milkman to his kin, is not especially helpful in either regard. He does not provide Milkman with the tools needed to navigate either the reality of his body or the social world that unwieldy body is forced to enter. From the outset, the first encounter that Milkman has with a man who might serve as the embodiment of his own future, Robert Smith, is one marked by catastrophe, by a public failure that ultimately ends in tragedy. The event leaves Milkman's imagination "bereft," robbing him of the joy that would naturally attend watching a man fly, as well as the possibility of such flight, such freedom, for his future self. Morrison's characterization of the Smith crash as an event that not only captures the attention of the community but also, in a slightly different register, captures any sense of potential or possibility, stealing it from Milkman before he is old enough to glean that sort of disappointment from personal experience, is critical. As presented, this is the first lesson Milkman ever learns about what it means to move through the world, the first time he projects his own experiences onto another and dares to see himself where he is not. In this sense, Robert Smith's death is not only a mirror for Milkman but also a kind of mirror stage:

> It suffices to understand the mirror stage in this context *as an identification*, in the full sense analysis gives to the term: namely, the transformation that takes place in the subject when he assumes [*assume*] an image—an image that is seemingly predestined to have an effect at this phase, as witnessed by the use in analytic theory of antiquity's term, "imago."
>
> The jubilant assumption [*assomption*] of his specular image by the kind of being—still trapped in his motor impotence and nursling dependence—the little man is at the *infans* stage thus seems to me to manifest in an exemplary situation the symbolic matrix in which the *I* is precipitated in a primordial form, prior to being objectified in the dialectic of identification with the other, and before language restores to it, in the universal, its function as a subject.
>
> This form would, moreover, have to be called the "ideal-I"—if we wanted to translate it into a familiar register—in the sense that it will also be the root-stock of secondary identifications, this latter term subsuming the libidinal normalization functions. But the important point is that this form situates the agency known as the ego, prior to its social determination, in a fictional direction that will forever remain irreducible for any single individual or, rather, that will only asymptotically approach the subject's becoming, no matter how successful the dialectical syntheses by which he must resolve, as *I*, his discordance with his own reality.[14]

This passage from Jacques Lacan's "The Mirror Stage as Formative of the *I* Function" avails to us a peculiar sort of second insight into the initial encounter between Robert Smith's legacy—his "mark," as Morrison terms it—and Milkman Dead, a protocol for imagining, at the level of trauma and psychological development, what transpires when an infant's birth is inextricably linked to a man crashing to his demise right in front of him. Though Lacan's analysis is useful for its metaphorical breadth, I would like to read against the grain of it here so as to honor the particularity of the mirroring that passes between Milkman and Robert Smith, as I think it contains elements of the Lacanian mirror stage but ultimately drives the subject of the stage, the child glaring into the mirror, in a slightly divergent direction than Lacan's theory, as presented here, can account for. Though there is undoubtedly a certain identification that takes place between Milkman and Robert Smith, I would argue that Milkman spends much of *Song of Solomon* actively disinvesting in the illogical, seemingly spontaneous activity we see from Smith in the book's earliest scenes.

Milkman, like his father, Macon Dead II, is exceedingly practical. His emotions are primarily invested in what can be held or owned. Milkman does not see an "ideal-I" in Smith but rather an *anti-ideal-I*, a portent, a warning of what happens when one seeks to elide or evade the law. The image of Smith's beautiful, crashing body haunts Milkman. It stands in as a representative of all that he seeks to avoid, the risk of loving anything too much, even one's own freedom, and the various kinds of leaping or leaving that might attend such love. Milkman's unceasing practicality, which could also be read as willful avoidance, though certainly not a lack, of something like creativity or daring, is a result of this origin steeped in blood, this cracked mirror image staring back at him from when he first entered the world. *Song of Solomon* is full of this sort of troublesome mirroring, replete with figures that look to elders and see versions of themselves they desperately seek to evade. Thus, the disappointment inherent to this version of the mirror stage lies not in the asymptotic approach of an ideal that never arrives but in the disappointment of a reflection that is inescapable, a model that is marked by failure, the anti-ideal-I that is always already a haunting presence that is nonetheless enfleshed. It is, to use Lacan's language, "a fictional direction that will forever remain irreducible for any single individual or, rather, that will only asymptotically approach the subject's becoming" primarily in the sense that these images, these living reflections, are fixtures from which characters like Milkman are always on the run. The images approach asymptotically, without ever reaching the body of the onlooker, because that is as close as Milkman and others will allow them. Robert Smith is indeed a mirror, the kind that Milkman has no interest in confronting. Given the persistence of Milkman's desire to fly, a desire that manifests itself in a number of palpable ways toward the conclusion of the novel, this rejection—that is, of Robert Smith as origin narrative, as the chaos from which Milkman's world emerges—is a reasonable strategy, one that allows Milkman to conduct a relatively safe, bourgeois lifestyle without the threat of reckless dreaming. In *Song of Solomon*, the figure of the anti-ideal-I is, from the outset, inextricably linked to images that are not mere extensions of psyche but living persons that Morrison's characters must contend with. For Milkman, the image of Robert Smith failing to fly—which is also, it should be noted, a failure to keep a promise he made in the note pasted to the front of his home—is just such a point of contention, as well as of fraught identification, throughout the novel.

The weight of Smith's failure lingers and ultimately manifests itself in ways that mark Milkman even beyond the supposed peculiarity that is often remarked on during his childhood. Beyond what the narrator refers to as a certain dullness—which registers here not just as the absence or suppression of intelligence but also as a lack of color or vibrancy, a doubling that is especially important given the splendor of Robert Smith's sartorial performance the day of his failed flight and only gains more traction as the novel picks up speed, its color palette widening all the while—there remains the issue of Milkman's wounded imagination, the ways in which the Smith crash serves as a swift, irrefutable education on the relationship between black men and the limits of law. As Milkman soon learns, the algorithm is relatively simple: bucking the law courts a quick death and ultimately makes one's life ungrievable.[15] It is this weight, perhaps, the weight that attends the realization that he is neither bird nor airplane that is eventually bodied forth as what the narrator describes, in the first instance, as a stylized gait:

> By the time Milkman was fourteen he had noticed that one of
> his legs was shorter than the other. When he stood barefoot and
> straight as a pole, his left foot was about half an inch off the floor.
> So he never stood straight; he slouched or leaned or stood with a
> hip thrown out, and he never told anybody about it—ever. . . . It
> wasn't a limp—not at all—just the suggestion of one, but it looked
> like an affected walk, the strut of a very young man trying to appear more sophisticated than he was. It bothered him and he
> acquired movements and habits to disguise what to him was a
> burning defect. He sat with his left ankle on his right knee, never
> the other way around. And he danced each new dance with a curios stiff-legged step that the girls loved and the other boys
> eventually copied. The deformity was mostly in his mind. Mostly,

but not completely, for he did have shooting pains in that leg after several hours on a basketball court. He favored it, believed it was polio, and felt secretly connected to the late President Roosevelt for that reason. Even when everybody was raving about Truman because he had set up a Committee on Civil Rights, Milkman secretly preferred FDR and felt very close to him. Closer, in fact, to him than to his own father, for Macon had no imperfection and age seemed to strengthen him. Milkman feared his father, respected him, but knew, because of the leg, that he could never emulate him. So he differed from him as much as he dared. Macon was clean-shaven; Milkman was desperate for a mustache. Macon wore bow ties; Milkman wore four-in-hands. Macon didn't part his hair. Milkman had a part shaved into his. Macon hated tobacco; Milkman tried to put a cigarette in his mouth every fifteen minutes. Macon hoarded his money; Milkman gave his away. But he couldn't help sharing with Macon his love of good shoes and fine thin socks. And he did try, as his father's employee, to do the work the way Macon wanted it done.[16]

The difference Morrison posits here between an interpretation of Milkman's limp as a physical disability born of ailment or physical injury (for example, the narrator's invocation of polio and Milkman's ongoing affection for President Roosevelt) and the limp as a product of Milkman's fears or desires—that is, the limp as the embodied performance of his yearning for sophistication or undeniable cool—is of paramount importance. Such overperformance, such compensation in the face of deep hunger for intimate relation, is an indelible component of Milkman's persona throughout the text.

In the place of the vocalized expression of that sort of desire, what we see instead are the sorts of gestures that Morrison lists when she outlines the various ways that Milkman purposely diverges from his father so as to ease the pain of his distance. This is the conflict that an unapproachable, inimitable model such as Macon Dead II presents for Milkman. Up and through adulthood, all he can do is leap, and even that is done in vain. What remains in the interval between his initial mirror, his anti-ideal-I, Robert Smith, and the ideal he seeks to emulate, his father, Macon, is a space that never closes. Instead, that distance manifests itself as a weight that Milkman bears in his body. As Morrison characterizes their relationship, the distance between Milkman and Macon is enacted through both the heaviness implicit in the latter's everyday movement and also his sartorial choices and methods of self-care. This is an altogether different heaviness indexed by the incongruous movement of Milkman's legs, themselves a symbolic marker of difference between his own physique and that of Macon—who is described as having "an athlete's stride"—the heaviness of their irreconcilability, the impossibility of Milkman ever measuring up.[17] The singular weight of patriarchal lineage is one that Milkman, repeatedly, is unable to bear with any sort of ease or comfort. Even his nickname represents a departure from family tradition and is a source of great frustration for his father, who, though he never discovers its deeply troubling origin—that his mother breastfed the boy well into childhood—nonetheless regards the appellation with disgust, thinking it "dirty, intimate, and hot."[18]

One of the more compelling moments of Morrison's initial description of Milkman's gait is the imagery of him dancing, her claim that Milkman's affected walk was actually a source of pride and positive regard when he would attend parties or other public gatherings with his peers. This distinction is critical, not only for its resonance with a social model of disability in which disability is always already a social and environmental phenomenon and thus not so much an inherent trait as a mode of being in the world determined by one's direct surroundings, architecturally and otherwise, but also because of the backdrop against which it places Milkman's yearning for the acknowledgment and care of his father. When contrasted against the reality of Milkman's status as a figure of prominence in the local community, a young man who is adored and emulated by most of his peers, then, there is a slight shift in how we might read the negative affects that predominate his relationship with his father.

By all accounts, Milkman never registers the love of his friends as love. Like the affective labor of so many of the women in his life—as he is rather abruptly reminded by his sister Lena later on in the novel—their desire for relation is unimportant, even invisible to him.[19] Perhaps unsurprisingly, Morrison has remarked elsewhere on her ongoing interest in this well-documented experience of invisibility, or at least *the description* of this unique sort or sense of nonbelonging in white civil society as a kind of invisibility, on the part of black men. In a 2013 public conversation with Junot Díaz at the New York Public Library, Morrison went as far as to offer a bit of counter-Ellisonian critique toward this point, saying simply, "Invisible to whom? Not to me."[20] Yet and still we see the product of that *feeling-invisible* bodied forth in how Milkman behaves, the cavalier way that he treats those who are not his father, who, even when he is an object of anger, is always deemed worthy of engagement. Even when Milkman is in conflict with his father, he accounts for him, and it is this accounting, this singular focus, that strikes me as a Lacanian drive toward an ideal self, an endeavor that is ultimately fruitless and produces an ongoing psychic injury that is bodied forth in the way that Milkman, quite literally, moves through space. The effect of his initial disappointment in Robert Smith and the subsequent disappointment of his father's coldness is to deeply wound Milkman, as the failings of both men come to register as imposed, immutable limits on his own range of possible lives. That Milkman's feelings, indeed his very capacity for feeling, become manifest in such a profound and in this case readily visible way is part of a long-standing thought pattern in Morrison's work. *Song of Solomon* in particular is replete with characters that appear, almost, to feel *too much* in a given moment and indeed feel various emotions with such depth and power that everyday living becomes untenable labor. As Melissa Gregg and Gregory Seigworth remind us,

> Affect is in many ways synonymous with *force* or *forces of encounter*. . . . At once intimate and impersonal, affect *accumulates* across both relatedness and interruptions in relatedness, becoming a palimpsest of force-encounters traversing the ebbs and swells of intensities that pass between "bodies" (bodies defined not by an outer skin-envelope or other surface boundary but by their potential to reciprocate or co-participate in passages of affect). Bindings and unbindings, becomings and un-becomings, jarring disorientations and rhythmic attunements. Affect marks a body's *belonging* to a world of encounters or; a world's belonging to a body of encounters but also, in *non-belonging*, through all those far sadder (de)compositions of mutual in-compossibilities. Always there are ambiguous or "mixed" encounters that impinge and extrude for worse and for better, but (most usually) in-between.[21]

Song of Solomon's cast of characters amend and augment such a working definition of affect, as it is the social performance of their mutual affectedness, the intractable ways in which they are *publicly affected* by their feelings toward one another, that is of paramount importance. For Morrison, belonging or nonbelonging to the world is a matter of recognition, and care, of whether or not we can ultimately belong to those we desire to belong to, whether we can experience the goodness of loving and being loved back.[22] Affect is always on the move throughout *Song of Solomon*, but it is constantly working in both public and private space, always blurring the line between the inner life of a character and the way they are presented or present themselves to their fellow townspeople, friends, or family. Time and time again, we see the sheer force with which unrequited love unspools the central characters' lives, few in as drastic a fashion as a secondary character named Porter, whose initial appearance in the text is its own argument for the singular power of nonbelonging to warp one's relation to the public sphere. While leaning out an attic window, drunk and cradling a shotgun tightly but not too well, Porter speaks not only to his condition but also to that of many characters to follow:

> Tears streamed down his face and he cradled the barrel of the shotgun in his arms as though it were the woman he had been begging for, searching for, all his life. "Gimme hate, Lord," he whimpered. "I'll take hate any day. But don't give me love. I can't take no more love, Lord. I can't carry it. Just like Mr. Smith. He couldn't carry it. It's too heavy. Jesus, you know. You know all about it. Ain't it heavy? Jesus? Ain't love heavy? Don't you see, Lord? You own son couldn't carry it. If it killed Him, what You think it's gonna do to me?"[23]

Porter elaborates for us here, early in the text, a corroboration of Robert Smith's final claim, reiterating that it was love, and not a desire to die, that led to Smith jumping off the roof of Mercy. Porter goes as far as to pray for the removal of said love, calling it an unbearable burden, heaviness fit to kill. Like Robert Smith before him, Porter seeks out higher ground to make such a proclamation about the workings of love as force, as mass, itself a gesture toward the desire for ascension that marks both these men in their grandest moments of recognition. It is not the weight of love alone that Smith and Porter can no longer bear but also the peculiar burden of their social position, the daily anguish of being cast low while dreaming of a life marked by transcendence. Porter's great insight here is that the black men in the novel experience these weights not as counterbalancing forces but in fact as dual obstacles to the forms of flight that occupy their dreams. To configure love in such a fashion, not solely as a liberating force but also as a potential antipode to such a force, is to conjure an expansive set of questions about the nature of kinship, about what it means to desire that which can destroy just as easily as it can make or mend.

It is the weight that attends this double bind that produces not only Porter's misery, and Smith's desire to fly, but also Milkman's limp and obsession with appearance. His profound alienation from any robust engagement with the social world beyond what the people he encounters daily *can do for him* is in no small part a result of the ways in which his attempts at fulfilling his desire for love, as well as his desire to love, have ended in tragic failure: his love for flight reduced to a dead man broken against concrete, his love for his father devolved into rote obedience. Rather than delight in the manifold joys of the social, Milkman chooses instead to seek out a certain kind of patrilineal security, any stable reminder that he has roots, a place set aside for him, something that is his and only his, that can be owned and never taken. It is primarily in this sense, that is, in his relationship to private property and what he imagines private property makes possible, that Milkman most resembles his father. Their singular obsession with what they believe that ownership can provide, the world for which it serves as both lock and key, is what binds them. And it is the contrast between Milkman, Macon, and the women in the novel that makes the most prominent instances of bird imagery, and all that such imagery suggests in this text, especially poignant.

Put differently, more even than gender as a category of social difference, what separate the men and women in *Song of Solomon* are their expressed relationships to private property, what they believe that property ownership, as well as other forms of possession, opens up or forecloses as it pertains to the value of life as such, which is also to say, how property functions as a marker of their individual and collective personhood. The most compelling example of this divergence is found in Milkman's aunt and Macon's only sibling, Pilate Dead, and is on grand display during the first detailed interaction between Pilate and Milkman. After a brief exchange in which Pilate admonishes him for saying "hi" (which, according to Pilate, is something one only says to "pigs and sheep when you want em to move") instead of "hello," the reader is granted a sketch of his initial impression of his aunt, the outcast and local legend:[24]

> Shame had flooded him. He had expected to feel it, but not that kind; to be embarrassed, yes, but not that way. She was the one who was ugly, dirty, poor, and drunk. The queer aunt whom his

sixth-grade schoolmates teased him about and whom he hated
because he felt personally responsible for her ugliness, her poverty, her dirt, and her wine. Instead she was making fun of his
school, of his teachers, of him. And while she looked as poor as
everyone said she was, something was missing from her eyes that
should have confirmed it. Nor was she dirty; unkempt, yes, but
not dirty. The whites of her fingernails were like ivory. And unless
he knew absolutely nothing, this woman was definitely not drunk.
Of course she was anything but pretty, yet he knew he could have
watched her all day: the fingers pulling thread veins from the or-
ange sections, the berry-black lips that made her look as though
she wore make-up, the earring. . . . And when she stood up, he
all but gasped. She was as tall as his father, and head and shoulders taller than himself. . . . She opened the door and they fol-
lowed her into a large sunny room that looked both barren and
cluttered. A moss-green sack hung from the ceiling. Candles
were stuck in bottles everywhere; newspaper articles and magazine pictures were nailed to the walls. But other than a rocking
chair, two straight-backed chairs, a large table, a sink and stove,
there was no furniture. Pervading everything was the odor of
pine and fermenting fruit.[25]

In a sense, Pilate's home operates as an extension of her persona:
the smell of fruit, its general unkemptness, and the emphasis on
the beauty of interpersonal interaction over respectable presenta-
tion all serving as contributing factors to the sense of surprise that
Milkman feels upon their first meeting.

The shame that Milkman experiences is a direct product of
Pilate's presence. Her everyday life doubles as a critique of his own.
Put somewhat differently, Pilate's willingness to carry on as she

does works in direct opposition to all that Milkman has been taught to hold dear. Her house does not serve as a marker of hard-earned wealth or middle-class status. Rather, her home is a living space in every other sense of the term. It is a venue for gathering and flourishing, for fleshly abundance with no regulatory force in place to curtail its song. That Pilate's house is also a house full of women—she lives with her two daughters, Hagar and Reba—is of central importance here; the absence of a dominant patriarch comes to index the absence of the desire for patriarchal codes of honor, order, and power. Hence, the black feminine comes to mark the possibility of another orientation in and toward the social world altogether in *Song of Solomon*, Pilate's unwieldy, unruly household providing the reader with a view of what an alternative domesticity might look like, one centered around invention and the production of pleasure instead of regulation or the maintenance of the current social order.

In contrast to a character like Macon Dead II, who has built his entire life on charging others to live, going from house to house demanding that he be paid on time so that he might continue to amass his fortune as others struggle to live from day to day, Pilate stands out as a fugitive from normative ways of thinking about what counts as honest work or labor worth living into. Much to Milkman's surprise, she is poor and yet unashamed, unkempt and yet willing to comport herself with an indifference that belies her class position. The material wealth that Macon has spent his life pursuing—and, indeed, has trained his son to pursue with similar tenacity—holds no weight for Pilate. This lack of interest in material wealth and its trappings is bodied forth in both her self-presentation and the home she keeps, a home that is largely devoid of saleable commodities but fit to burst with laughter, luck, love.[26] She mocks the world that Milkman comes from not out of envy but out of what might be better described as a kind of confusion. Her insight into the restrictive character of a life centrally concerned with accumulation serves to destabilize the appeal of such a lifestyle for both Milkman and the reader. Her every move indexes the possibility of another world.

At no point is the clash between Macon Dead II's hypercapitalist ethos and the lovely chaos of Pilate Dead's life philosophy more palpable than in Macon's eventual plan to rob his sister once he discerns—calling, in that moment of realization, on a long-past skirmish-turned-lethal with an elderly stranger in a cave—that the aforementioned "moss-green sack hung from the ceiling" is actually filled with a dead man's gold. From the outset, the heist appears to be a doomed mission, though it is not without its share of wonder:

> Milkman stared off into the sky for inspiration, and while glancing toward the rooftops of the used-car places, he saw a white peacock poised on the roof of a long low building that served as headquarters for Nelson Buick. He was about to accept the presence of the bird as one of those waking dreams he was subject to whenever indecisiveness was confronted with reality, when Guitar opened his eyes and said "Goddam! Where'd that come from?"
>
> Milkman was relieved. "Must of come from the zoo."
>
> "That raggedy-ass zoo? Ain't nothing in there but two tired monkeys and some snakes."
>
> "Well, where then?"

"Beats me."

"Look—she's flying down." Milkman felt again his unre-
strained joy at anything that could fly. "Some jive flying, but
look at her strut."

"He."

"Huh?"

"He. That's a he. The male is the only one got that tail full of
jewelry. Son of a bitch. Look at that." The peacock opened its tail
wide. "Let's catch it. Come on, Milk," and Guitar started to run
toward the fence. . . .

"How come it can't fly no better than a chicken?" Milkman
asked.

"Too much tail. All that jewelry weighs it down. Like vanity.
Can't nobody fly with all that shit. Wanna fly, you got to give up
the shit that weighs you down."

The peacock jumped onto the hood of the Buick and once
more spread its tail, sending the flashy Buick into oblivion.[27]

In contradistinction to the failed flight that opens the novel, what
Morrison presents here, through the body of the white peacock, is
an image of flight that occupies a kind of middle ground, a "jive
flying," an airborne strut that conveys pride while also operating
as a performance of irreparable limitation. In a symbolic register,
the white peacock in this scene enacts a confidence that belies its
position in the social world of birds, its weighted, belabored ascension a mere shadow of other birds' capacity for flight. As Guitar
so astutely points out in the preceding passage, the peacock is a
bird that wants to soar, and tries with all its might to achieve liftoff,
but never succeeds.

In this scene, the peacock operates as an evocative stand-in for any number of male characters the reader encounters throughout *Song of Solomon*, the conflict between its desire for flight—that is, flight as both egress and ascension—and all that weighs it down serving as the grounds for such symbolic slippage. For Milkman and Guitar, mocking the peacock and chasing it—at one point, Milkman even jokes that they should eat it—doubles as a moment of unconscious self-critique, as many of their criticisms of the peacock could just as easily be directed at their own lives. Milkman and Guitar too are figures that try over and over to achieve flight only to fail in one way or another. For Guitar, such freedom is bound up with seeking redress for the extrajudicial killing of African Americans through his work with the Seven Days, a secret society devoted to killing one random white person for every black person unjustly slain. For Milkman, the metaphor is much more direct. Not unlike his father, Milkman is weighed down by both his desire for material wealth as and the various material comforts that he already has available to him, comforts that have helped produce the exact sort of vanity Guitar sees in the peacock. Not unlike Robert Smith, the white peacock is yet another anti-ideal mirror against which Milkman is forced to engage, consciously or otherwise, with the full weight of what holds him back, with how untenable his dreams appear against a world ruled by the law of gravity, the law of graves.

The white peacock is also, in this vein, a representative of the normative white masculinity that Guitar and Milkman desire for themselves. Guitar's joke about catching and eating the peacock seems to support such a reading of this scene. His desire to consume the animal is also his desire to simultaneously mesh with it and destroy it, to make it a part of his body, have it pass into and fill him. By the passage's end, the white peacock is all Milkman and Guitar can see, its white tail having sent "the flashy Buick into oblivion." Their desire for what the peacock represents, even as they mock it, blots out all else. The tension implicit in such desire, in the pair's jeering, which is inextricable from both the discomfort and the awe they feel in the presence of such a beautiful creature— think here about Guitar's implicit claim that such a wondrous animal could never have come from their local, underfunded zoo, a zoo that boasts only a couple of monkeys and some snakes, common beasts, nothing worthy of visitation or praise—is illuminating. The pair's resentment for the peacock is also a kind of reverence. Because they cannot touch it, cannot become it, they mock its freedom to move, its capacity for flight. Think here of how the Buick is sent "into oblivion," by the expansive reach of the peacock's tail, how the peacock's beauty obscures the Buick, this ideal commodity, as a site of desire altogether. In lieu of the car, Milkman and Guitar yearn either to consume or denigrate the white peacock, to dominate it. This yearning that is also refusal, hatred, adoration, and envy reflects well the forms of aspirational masculinity that Milkman enacts and embodies throughout the text. At every turn, there is an ongoing struggle between the complexity of what he feels and the narrowness of the world available to him, which makes this performance always seem like an act of desperation or survival tactic. Rather than appear as yet another illusion inspired by the ongoing conflict between "indecisiveness" and "reality" that marks Milkman's young adulthood, the peacock serves as a grand reminder of the young men's joint purpose, the heist that will make it so that they too might be visible, dazzling, valuable enough to send anything else beautiful into oblivion:

But the bird had set them up. Instead of continuing the argument about how they would cop, they began to fantasize about
what the gold could buy when it became legal tender. Guitar, es-
chewing his recent asceticism, allowed himself the pleasure of
waking up old dreams: what he would buy for his grandmother
and her brother, Uncle Billy, the one who had come up from
Florida to help raise them all after his father died; the marker he
would buy for his father's grave, "pink with lilies carved on it";
then stuff for his brother and sisters, and his sisters' children.
Milkman fantasized too, but not for the stationary things Guitar
described. Milkman wanted boats, cars, airplanes, and the command of a large crew. He would be whimsical, generous, myste-
rious with the money. But all the time he was laughing and going
on about what he would do and how he planned to live, he was
aware of the falseness in his voice. He wanted the money—
desperately, he believed—but other than making tracks out of
the city, far away from Not Doctor Street, and Sonny's Shop, and
Mary's Place, and Hagar, he could not visualize a life that much
different from the one he had. New people. New places. Command. That was what he wanted for his life. . . . He screamed and
shouted "Wooeeeee!" at Guitar's list, but because his life was not
unpleasant and even had a certain amount of luxury in addition
to its comfort, he felt off center. He just wanted to beat a path
away from his parents' past, which was also their present and
which was threatening to become his present as well.[28]

The figure of the anti-ideal-I shows up not in the crashing body of
Robert Smith here but in the form of Milkman's parents. During
a moment of intense, shared clarity with Guitar about what he
would do if he had all the material resources he had ever wanted,

all Milkman can think of is the possibility of plotting an escape route from the life he has now. Rather than some grand purchase or marker of individual wealth, what Milkman seems to want more than anything else is a trap door, an accessible point of egress that will allow him to avoid the image he sees staring back with startling clarity from the white peacock's inimitable glow: a life marked by material comfort but a lack of meaningful relation.

Still, what more can we make of the white peacock's whiteness? How do we read the clear, chromatic distinction between the animal figure positioned here as a representative of the "jive flying" that characterizes black male social life and its implicit relationship to failure, on the one hand, and the transcendent white masculinity that circumscribes that life and provides a context wherein such failure registers as failure for the two black male characters in the scene, on the other? How does the peacock's whiteness complicate its viability as a symbol for black men's experience of patriarchal masculinity, their straining against it and striving toward it? Here, Frantz Fanon's insight on white gaze and black male experience is instructive: "I arrive slowly in the world; sudden emergences are no longer my habit. I crawl along. The white gaze, the only valid one, is already dissecting me. I am fixed. Once their microtomes are sharpened, the whites objectively cut sections of my reality. I have been betrayed. I sense, I see in this white gaze that it's the arrival not of a new man, but of a new type of man, a new species. A Negro, in fact!"[29] Fanon's recourse to the language of both *validity* and *fixedness* is helpful here and further elucidates the symbolic work of the peacock in this scene. The fixedness that Fanon describes, an immobility produced by the intractable gaze of white civil society, is inextricable from the wonder that Milkman and Guitar experience in this moment, the way that the white peacock arrests their line of vision, demands their attention, and ultimately spurs them to dream of obtaining wealth unlike anything they have seen before. It is the validity of the white gaze, which is also to say, the seeming inescapability of whiteness *as a primary source of legitimate validation* for Milkman and Guitar, that anchors this scene. Once confronted with the singular white object, the two forget themselves and ultimately get lost in the fantasy of having what, to their minds, whiteness has within it: riches, social access, the capacity to provide for their families.

What would necessarily attend such a reading is an engagement with what it means that the white peacock, even as a metaphorical stand-in for whiteness, cannot fly any "better than a chicken." In this sense, Morrison's white peacock is a signifier that comes with a critique of the signified built right in. From the moment the peacock appears, the notion of whiteness as pure transcendence is already unsettled. The white peacock flies no better than any other bird and is thus a fraught, imperfect site of aspiration. It too is laid low by vanity.

Milkman's experiences with his family throughout *Song of Solomon* reflect this broader obsession with prestige and the wages of whiteness.[30] In lieu of a more nurturing familial experience, what Milkman received instead was an inviolable set of rules about the proper relations between men and the world as an ongoing conflict rooted in property and possession, in domination as a desirable mode of relation, and value as that which is found in human lives only to the extent that those lives can be leveraged for material gain or social status. In Milkman's case, such ways of thinking are legible primarily through the figure of the inheritance. For his entire life, the relationship between his parents, as well as between his father and the other residents of Not Doctor Street, was always a hierarchy grounded in the accrual of material goods. Even his parents' marriage was, in a sense, always at its core an attempt by his father to move up in the world, to soar as best he could. The consequences of this weight, as well as this general orientation toward personal worth as an object that can only be attained through market relations, is made manifest in the moment when Milkman is called on by the peacock's presence to indulge in his wildest dreams and can come up with nothing worth telling. Rather than imagine a world made new by access to unlimited capital, Milkman can only praise the vision that his best friend calls forth. This moment doubles as a critique, one might imagine, of Morrison's broader argument in *Song of Solomon* about what a single-minded commitment to the pursuit of material wealth can make of a person.[31]

Thus, when a passerby early on in the novel says of Macon Dead II that "a nigger in business is a terrible thing to see," the criticism is less about Macon himself and more about a relentless critique throughout the novel of material wealth as a useful marker of one's beauty, intellect, or value. For Morrison, there are any number of other ways of thinking about value that have little or nothing to do with monetary gain, approaches that are exemplified in the way that Pilate Dead carries out her everyday life. Indeed, the ongoing conflict between Macon and Pilate can be thought of as a matter not only of personal disagreement between two siblings, with much of the ill will, of course, residing on Macon's side of things, but also of philosophical irreconcilability, a clash of values embodied in their personal (for example, the way that Pilate raises Hagar and Reba versus the way Macon raises Lena, First Corinthians, and Milkman) and professional (Pilate as self-employed purveyor of wine versus Macon as landlord) lives. Milkman's yearning for something more, something beyond what he has been raised to see value in, establishes him as a point of intersection between Macon and Pilate. He desires the sort of freedom that Pilate's lifestyle makes possible but is also wedded to the comfort and social cachet of Macon's approach.

For Milkman, the desire to shirk his parents' present is also the desire to forgo the false promise of the nuclear family and upper-middle-class social status in favor of the unknown. As Morrison later makes clear, doing so will require that he go in search of something other than the lifestyle, and the legacy, that he has inherited from Macon. It will require him to seek out new modes of thinking relation beyond what patriarchy promises, something other than birthright or dominion. Rather tragically, Milkman's quest for this sort of freedom, which is ultimately nothing other than freedom from the life his father has chosen, is inextricable from a plan that his father has laid out for him, a plan to steal the gold he believes Pilate has hanging from her ceiling. That this sack of gold turns out be little more than a bag full of human bones is a compelling, perverse turn. That said bones once belonged to Milkman's godfather shifts the entire narrative in a wildly different direction. Now, instead of Milkman plotting a line of flight away from his father's past, he will give all of himself to grasping a fuller picture of it. Rather than seek his own fortune, he will take on a different sort of journey altogether, an odyssey in the name of the Father.

❁

The metonymic relationship between flying and black fatherhood in *Song of Solomon* is an elaborate one for Morrison, a coupling intended to convey a familiar message that might initially ring as

dangerously close to something like pathology but nonetheless dis-
plays radical potential for the way it allows us to read the ways
that gender, blackness, and kinship are at work in the text. In a
1977 interview with Mel Watkins, Morrison states, "This book was
different. . . . Men are more prominent. They interested me in a
way I hadn't thought about before, almost as a species. I used what
I knew, what I'd heard. But I had to think of becoming a whole
person in masculine terms, so there were craft problems. I couldn't
use the metaphors I'd used describing women. I needed something
that suggested dominion—a different kind of drive."[32] This line of
thinking is further developed later on in the interview:

> That's why flying is the central metaphor in *Song*—the literal
> taking off and flying into the air, which is everybody's dream. My
> children used to talk about it all the time—they were amazed
> when they found they couldn't fly. They took it for granted that
> all they had to do was jump up and flap their arms. I used it not
> only in the African sense of whirling dervishes and getting out
> of one's skin, but also in the majestic sense of a man who goes
> too far, whose adventures take him far away . . . black men travel,
> they split, they get on trains, they walk, they move. I used to hear
> those old men talk about traveling—which is not getting from
> here to there, it's the process—they even named themselves after
> trains. It's a part of black life, a positive, majestic thing, but there
> is a price to pay—the price is children. The fathers may soar, they
> may triumph, they may leave, but the children know who they
> are; they remember, half in glory and half in accusation. That is
> one of the points of *Song*: all the men have left someone, and it
> is the children who remember it, sing about it, mythologize it,
> make it a part of their family history.[33]

What do we make of the seeming paradox that Morrison lays out here? After leading off with the claim that the abundance of male characters in *Song of Solomon* pushed her to deploy an entirely different type of metaphors than she had in her first two novels, *The Bluest Eye* and *Sula*, metaphors implicitly tied to what we might think of, following Morrison, as a certain drive toward *dominion*, Morrison then pivots toward a characterization of the men in her novels as marked by an insatiable wanderlust. Though these dual visions of the male characters in *Song of Solomon* are in no way irreconcilable, they do present a compelling conflict. How does one singularly concerned with escape also live a life driven by the desire for dominion? And what does dominion mean for the specific subset of men whose lives Morrison is committed to exploring, men with very little access to traditional methods of accruing social status or power?

For these men, it appears, flight or, to use Morrison's term, *travel* is the primary means by which to achieve something resembling power or possession. For these ostensibly failed men, men who can never own much of anything, can never quite live into dominance or dominion as a viable mode of relation, travel, and the absence from the home that naturally attends travel, perhaps also becomes a means of asserting control, of offering proof that they *matter*, in every sense of the term. In a related vein, that Morrison frames her concern with black male characterization as a matter of species is a fascinating choice and would appear, on the surface, to reify a certain kind of gender essentialism. What such a reading would necessarily elide, however, is what Morrison's framing of black gender study as *species thinking* elucidates about the undeniable relationship between the practice of taxonomy and what Alexander Weheliye writes about the law's tendency to "recognize the humanity of racialized subjects only in the restricted idiom of personhood-as-ownership."[34] If personhood is tethered to ownership, of both one's body and various forms of nonhuman, nonliving property, then what do we call the men whom Morrison cites as her primary inspiration for the men in *Song of Solomon*, men who own little or nothing? How do we understand their personhood, over and against a world that categorically denies it and indeed enforces such denial through everyday forms of violence and surveillance?

The movement that Morrison gives voice to here, the desire to travel, to avoid being seen or held down, avails itself as a potential mode of thinking fugitivity through the pathology of the absent black father, who, as we see from the characterizations of black fathers that abound throughout *Song of Solomon*, is cast as absent even when he is present or is present in forms of orature or spectral matter *even when he is physically gone*. The black men in *Song of Solomon* trouble traditional ways of thinking about the dichotomy of absence and presence and ultimately unsettle prevailing stereotypes about black paternity, including those that appear to animate Morrison's earlier quoted commentary. Even a generous reading of these comments would have to account for the framing of *Song of Solomon* as a text in which "all the men have left someone" and its connection to an antiquated discourse of black fatherhood as a paradox of sorts, a social institution that is in persistent peril and through which many of the other, myriad problems that come to represent the lived experience of blackness in the United States can be traced and ultimately explained. The oft-cited 1965 study *The Negro Family: The Case for National Action*, commonly referred to as the "Moynihan Report," is illuminating in this regard:

In essence, the Negro community has been forced into a matriarchal structure which, because it is so out of line with the rest
of the American society, seriously retards the progress of the
group as a whole, and imposes a crushing burden on the Negro
male and, in consequence, on a great many Negro women as well.

There is, presumably, no special reason why a society in which
males are dominant in family relationships is to be preferred to a
matriarchal arrangement. However, it is clearly a disadvantage
for a minority group to be operating on one principle, while the
great majority of the population, and the one with the most ad-
vantages to begin with, is operating on another. This is the present situation of the Negro. Ours is a society which presumes
male leadership in private and public affairs. The arrangements
of society facilitate such leadership and reward it. A subculture,
such as that of the Negro American, in which this is not the pattern, is placed at a distinct disadvantage.[35]

This excerpt, taken from "The Tangle of Pathology" portion of the
report, lays out a number of the document's core principles. Moynihan's argument here certainly includes elements of Morrison's
characterization of black men as habitually absent from their
children's lives—though she ascribes such absence to a yearning
for adventure rather any sort of reaction to structural violence—but,
in stark comparison to Morrison, Moynihan's critical aim then
lands squarely on the black women who are forced to care for the
family units that these particular men leave in their wake.

Though Moynihan is certainly concerned with what he calls
"desertion" *as such*—a concern that, it should be noted, is vividly
illustrated in passages such as the following: "As a direct result of
this high rate of divorce, separation, and desertion, a very large

percent of Negro families are headed by females. While the percentage of such families among whites has been dropping since 1940, it has been rising among Negroes"—his primary interest lies elsewhere, specifically in the irremediable danger of the matriarchal figure.[36] For Moynihan, black mothers not only represent the foreclosure of the possibility of black inclusion on a broader social scale, hence the "distinct disadvantage" he invokes toward the end of the passage, but are also directly culpable for a much deeper set of interpersonal conflicts between themselves and the black men in their lives. The "crushing burden" that Moynihan describes operates in this passage and beyond as subtext, as yet another explanation for the flight of the black men who serve as the report's central object of concern. There is a legible desire throughout the report to interrogate and ultimately repair what Moynihan deems to be the broken order of things in black households. This desire, one imagines, is linked to a larger concern not only about the collective future of black men specifically but also about the unique threat to prevailing gender norms that the presence of these particular black women present. This pervasive fear is architectonic: the threat of black women as the heads of black American households not only is what holds much of Moynihan's argument together but also, at the level of feeling, seems intended to generate the concern that we see conveyed in the document's title, the concern that necessarily attends any call for national action. The document itself doubles as an extensive performance of white male anxiety over what black families mean for the very notion of family as a stable object, how black families, if left unchecked, might erode the conceptual underpinnings of the nuclear family as a national institution.

For Moynihan, then, the black male subjects of the report are rendered powerless, and ultimately broken, not only by unrelenting and largely invisible systems of structural violence but also by the black women closest to them:

> The effect on family functioning and role performance of this historical experience [economic deprivation] is what you might predict. Both as a husband and as a father the Negro male is made to feel inadequate, not because he is unlovable or unaffectionate, lacks intelligence or even a gray flannel suit. But in a society that measures a man by the size of his pay check, he doesn't stand very tall in a comparison with his white counterpart. To this situation he may react with withdrawal, bitterness toward society, aggression both within the family and racial group, self-hatred, or crime. Or he may escape through a number of avenues that help him to lose himself in fantasy or to compensate for his low status through a variety of exploits.[37]

The vision of black men presented in this portion of the Moynihan Report is far afield of what Morrison describes. Still, what remains worthy of note here is Moynihan's gesture toward the psychic toll that the capitalist character of white civil society takes on black men, a toll that Morrison not only accounts for but posits as a central conflict in *Song of Solomon,* though without resorting to the sort of imprecise theorizing on grand display in the Moynihan Report. Morrison sees pride, and even vanity, where Moynihan sees only despair and despondence, men who are unable to *strut,* which is, for him, "the very essence of the male animal."[38] Again, black masculinity appears here as a problem of species, of how to account for these men who are not men, men who are "holes," to use Lewis Gordon's language, and thus not only nonhuman but also devoid of meaningful content.[39] Though critical differences abound, it should be noted that Morrison and Moynihan alike respond to the same phenomenon: the despair produced by the promise of a normative masculinity, the promise that is by its very nature unrealizable and especially so for black men like the ones Morrison describes, men who must daily confront the reality of their own social and economic fixity, a fixity that doubles as a kind of disqualification from the province of the properly masculine.

For Moynihan, the crisis of black masculinity must be the primary object of our critical energies. Everything else, from disparities in educational attainment to underemployment, is posited as either a direct cause or result of this phenomenon. Morrison too sees black men's desire for an elsewhere, and the flight from home that is commonly cast as its direct product, as an issue that profoundly affects black social life, and yet, in stark contrast to Moynihan, she posits this leaving as "a positive, majestic thing" rather than as a pervasive social ill.

Placing Moynihan to the side for a moment, what are we to make of such a claim on Morrison's part? How do we reconcile the waves of critical attention devoted to the supposed ubiquity of the black absentee father with Morrison's contention here that fathers' search for another life might be a much more complex affair, one greeted with a certain ambivalence even by their children, who remember them "half in glory and half in accusation"?[40] Morrison's argument that the children of the men in question turn their lives into stories, and myths in particular, once they leave is worth our attention and is echoed in David Marriott's *On Black Men*. Marriott writes,

> Hence the mark that the black father leaves, a mark that is both ineffaceable and irremediable. Typed, in the wider culture, as the cause of, and cure for, black men's "failure," his father's appar-

ently lost, and untellable, life is the story that the son must find and narrate if he is to begin to understand how, and why, blackness has come to represent an inheritable fault. . . . "What is wrong with black fathers? What is wrong with black men?": these questions loom over postwar American culture, part of a more pervasive anxiety about the decline of paternal authority, the so-called "crisis" of masculinity in contemporary cultural life. A monumental crisis: for black men, the despair of living knowing that life itself is always in question, interfered with, disrupted.[41]

In Marriott, as in Morrison and Moynihan, the black father appears as a figure of tremendous social import on the national scale. Through the body of the always already absent black father, social anxiety is eased or elevated, policy changes come into being, prisons are built. For Marriott, it is the role of the son to tell the father's story and to use that narrative as a means through which he might navigate a world that hates him just as it hated his father, that calls his father's presence an illusion, his absence an inevitability. The question remains: What becomes of black women when black families, and black social life in a broader sense, are conceived of primarily in these terms? How might we craft a mode of reading and being together in the world that can account for the divergent ways in which white-supremacist patriarchy acts *differently*, though always simultaneously, even and especially under the guise of material benefit, on black men and black women?

On this front, I want to turn to a 1984 conversation between James Baldwin and Audre Lorde held in the pages of *Essence* magazine:

> *JB:* Do you know what happens to a man when he's ashamed of himself when he can't find a job? When his socks stink?

When he can't protect anybody? When he can't do anything? Do you know what happens to a man when he
can't face his children because he's ashamed of himself?
It's not like being a woman . . .

AL: No, that's right. Do you know what happens to a woman who
gives birth, who puts that child out there and has to go out
and hook to feed it? Do you know what happens to a woman
who goes crazy and beats her kids across the room because
she's so full of frustration and anger? Do you know what that
is? Do you know what happens to a lesbian who sees her
woman and her child beaten on the street while six other
guys are holding her? Do you know what that feels like?[42]

What emerges from the dynamic tension of Baldwin's and Lorde's
positions in this passage is a toolbox for rethinking a number of
the central conflicts not only in *Song of Solomon* but in Morrison's
entire corpus, conflicts staged over gender and energized by the
central question of what it means not only to suffer but to suffer
solely *because* one is black and not yet dead, because of a black feminine or black masculine identification that is marked as a site of
danger in need of regulatory force. What the conversation between
Lorde and Baldwin here brings to the fore are the ways in which
either position is rendered incommunicable, at least in part, because
of the scale at which the particular forms of violence being discussed take place.[43] The kinds of ongoing, structural violation described by both authors stand out from this passage as an impasse
that appears too high to get over, too wide to get around. As both
their conversation and the repeated inter- and intragender conflicts
in *Song of Solomon* make plain, there is a deep-seated anguish here
that must be accounted for in a conversation about the tragic in-

terplay between black social life and antiblack social systems, the need for a more robust language with which to analyze the sorts of interpersonal turmoil that both Lorde and Baldwin describe.

What becomes clear by the interview's end is that Baldwin and Lorde—operating here as representative figures of sorts, though certainly not in any totalizing or comprehensive fashion—do not and perhaps *cannot* fully comprehend each other's struggles at the level of experience, largely because there is a fundamental difference at play in terms of how their respective battles against patriarchy are structured, a difference that requires something other than an uncomplicated vision of black empowerment that would elide gender particularity in the name of racial uplift. What the conversation between Lorde and Baldwin emphasizes, and in its best moments enacts, is an empathy that Moynihan simply cannot fathom, an empathy that materializes as an ongoing engagement with the everyday experiences of black women and black men and ultimately produces a space of radical co-laboring within the conversation itself, an exchange that is something other than and in excess of the violent division Moynihan describes.

Baldwin's invocation of the ways in which predatory capitalism operates in the everyday as a persistent assault on the pride of black men signals a return to the set of questions Morrison implicitly lays out in describing the men who inspired *Song of Solomon*. For the black men who cannot derive their sense of pride from traditional modes of accruing and maintaining wealth, there must be alternative means of producing self-esteem and dignity, modes that, for Morrison, are often linked to movement, changing names, being, in every meaningful sense, untouchable. This tension between black fatherhood and flight, which is at its core a conflict staged over names, the family name, the name of the son who mythologizes the father, renaming him and thus making him his own, is in no place more vivid in *Song of Solomon* than in the text's final movement, during Milkman's journey to Shalimar, the small town where he hopes to unearth the family history that has eluded him up to this point in the novel. Milkman succeeds in this goal, ultimately decrypting an old fable that all the town's children sing en route to coming upon, in a conversation with a local resident by the name of Susan Byrd, the backstory of the charismatic black male figure around whom the entire town, and in some ways the entire text, has been built:

"Why did you call Solomon a flying African?"

"Oh, that's just some old folks' lie they tell around here. Some of those Africans they brought over here as slaves could fly. A lot of them flew back to Africa. The one around here who did was this same Solomon, or Shalimar—I never knew which was right. He had a slew of children, all over the place. You may have noticed that everybody around here claims kin to him. Must be over forty families spread in these hills calling themselves Solomon something or other. I guess he must have been hot stuff." She laughed. "But anyway, hot stuff or not, he disappeared and left everybody. Wife, everybody, including some twenty-one children. And they say they all saw him go. The wife saw him and the children saw him. They were all working in the fields. They used to try to grow cotton here. Can you imagine? In these hills? . . . Well, back to this Jake boy. He was supposed to be one of Solomon's original twenty-one—all boys and all of them with the same mother. Jake was the baby. The baby and the wife were next to him when he flew off."

"When you say 'flew off' you mean he ran away, don't you? Escaped?"

"No, I mean flew. Oh, it just foolishness, you know, but according to the story he wasn't running away. He was flying. He flew. You know, like a bird. Just stood up in the fields one day, ran up some hill, spun around a couple of times, and was lifted up in the air. Went right on back to wherever it was he came from. There's a big double-headed rock over the valley named for him. It like to killed the woman, the wife. I guess you could say 'wife.' Anyway she's supposed to have screamed out loud for days. And there's a ravine near here they call Ryna's Gulch, and sometimes you can hear this funny sound by it that the wind makes. People say it's the wife, Solomon's wife, crying. Her name was Ryna. They say she screamed and screamed, lost her mind completely. You don't hear about women like that anymore, but there used to be more—the kind of woman that couldn't live without a particular man. And when the man left, they lost their minds, or died or something. Love, I guess. But I always thought it was trying to take care of children by themselves, you know what I mean?"[44]

Here, in Susan Byrd's retelling of an age-old local myth, we hear an echo of Porter's lament earlier in the novel, his desire to be released from the heaviness of love lest it crush him. By the end of her account, Susan Byrd's vision of Solomon's life reads not only as a moment of clarification but as an encapsulation of the novel's larger themes: black men's pride, their desire for flight, and how both complicate and contaminate the possibilities of a more normative vision of black fatherhood. As is the case elsewhere in Morrison's oeuvre, there is a profound empathy for black men in this moment from Morrison, an empathy that does not require her to put black women's experiences under erasure.

In this scene of origin, the moment when Solomon is finally unveiled, he is depicted as both singularly elegant and thoroughly delinquent, "hot stuff" to the point that an entire town desires to be associated with him, but ultimately selfish enough to leave everyone he loves behind in the name of self-possession. Not unlike Milkman, Solomon, it would appear, values his own mobility more than he does the loved ones whose invisible labor makes his very life possible. It is this willingness to pursue freedom at all costs that is Milkman's true inheritance from Solomon and Macon and Robert Smith alike, all of whom did not hesitate to put their own desires—whether it was for love or property or an elsewhere they could neither name nor touch—before the direct needs of their families. Ryna, Ruth, Lena, First Corinthians, Hagar, Pilate: all lose their lives in one way or another, either to the grave or to a kind of quiet, internal death, for the sake of the men whose failure to fly—desperate as they might be for an exit, an exhale— constitutes the grounds of their identity. For Morrison, this is the central conflict of the black masculine: this love that feels like heaviness, this sense of always being watched. From this angle, the oft-repeated claim throughout the book that "everybody wants the life of a black man" appears not only as a claim about a social world in which black men are made hypervisible as both objects of sexual desire and threats to the safety of the public at large but also as a gesture toward the inner life of the black men in the novel, black men who feel wanted but never fully known.[45] In *Song of Solomon*, what emerges from such yearning is a tendency toward abandonment and a persistent choosing of certain forms of male kinship (friend-friend, father-son, even stranger-stranger) over relation-

ships to and with women that might extend beyond the erotic or
the extractive.[46]

When Milkman is finally able to walk without limping, we are
led to believe that he has been transformed by the pride he feels
after the doe hunt, a pride derived from the company and praise
of other men.[47] The natural continuation of this metaphor, the moment he learns to fly, is also linked to his relationship with other
men in the text, not only Solomon but also Guitar. Juxtaposed
against the specter of Pilate's dead body, herself slain at the hands
of a man who desired Milkman's life more than he ever cared about
hers or that of most other women outside of a certain sense of in-
traracial possession,[48] Milkman is able to soar, if only to fly "into
the killing arms of his brother."[49] Even in this final scene, a moment predicated on the seeming impossibility of a black male kinship bond that does not necessitate some form of violence—either
from civil society or from within the bond itself—there is nonetheless the trace of love, the heartbreak that drove Guitar, not unlike Hagar, to want to take Milkman's life once he suspected him
of betrayal. For Morrison, the black masculine is composed of all
these divergent elements operating in dynamic, dangerous tension.
It is this fear and this joy, this pain and this hunger, that anchor
the black masculine, though they do not represent its totality. To
the very end, these figures are complicated to the point of contradiction. They are ugly—and beautiful too.[50]

3

Mule

Work might be better conceptualized by examining the range of work that African-American women actually perform. Work as alienated labor can be economically exploitative, physically demanding, and intellectually deadening—the type of work long associated with Black women's status as "mule." Alienated labor can be paid—the case of Black women in domestic service, those Black women working as dishwashers, dry-cleaning assistants, cooks, and health-care assistants, as well as some professional Black women engaged in corporate mammy work; or it can be unpaid, as with the seemingly never-ending chores of many Black grandmothers and Black single mothers. But work can also be empowering and creative, even if it physically challenging and appears to be demeaning.

—Patricia Hill Collins, *Black Feminist Thought*

My principal question, phrased plainly, is: what different modalities of the human come to light if we do not take the liberal humanist figure of Man as the master-subject but focus on how humanity has been imagined and lived by those subjects excluded from this domain?

—Alexander G. Weheliye, *Habeas Viscus: Racializing Assemblages, Biopolitics, and Black Feminist Theories of the Human*

Let's face it. I am a marked woman, but not everybody knows
my name. "Peaches" and "Brown Sugar," "Sapphire" and "Earth
Mother," "Aunty," "Granny," God's "Holy Fool," a "Miss Ebony
First," or "Black Woman at the Podium": I describe a locus of
confounded identities, a meeting ground of investments and
privations in the national treasury of rhetorical wealth. My
country needs me, and if I were not here, I would have to be
invented.

—Hortense Spillers, "Mama's Baby, Papa's Maybe: An American
Grammar Book"

Throughout Zora Neale Hurston's corpus, we find any number
of moments marked by the presence of nonhuman animals
that buck expectations rooted in a normative zoological framework for creaturely behavior—consider the goat that flags a train
in *Mules and Men* or the revenge-seeking rattlesnake in her short
story "Sweat"—but nowhere is this desire to render the insurgent
potential of animal life more vividly on display than in her 1937
masterwork *Their Eyes Were Watching God*. Therein, Hurston crafts
a world in which animals perform species in a fashion that destabilizes and defamiliarizes normative expectations around not only
animal interiority but also animal *sociality*. My aim herein is to
offer an alternative reading of the way that the figure of the mule,
in particular, appears in the text, one that strains against the grain
of how the mule has historically been marked in twentieth-century
literary criticism and elsewhere, that is, as largely or *solely* a site of
gendered oppression, labor that is taken for granted and rendered
imperceptible. Though I will argue that these regulatory forces
are often at work when the mule appears on the scene as a signifier, I will also argue that such forces are never the totality of what

is present, that muleness indeed represents otherworldly duress but also the potential for an otherwise world, that is, a radically different set of social and political relations, in the midst of and in spite of that constraint.

Hence, what follows is an extended reading of the way that muleness moves through the text as an analytic of power, how Hurston returns to the figure of the mule again and again—sometimes even when there are no mules *as such* present in a given scene—in order to elucidate the power relations that produce the mule as a form of animal life, which is also to say, a creature invented *for the sake of labor and labor alone,* as well as a useful metonym for describing the experiences of black women living under patriarchy's unremitting pressures. Through a close reading of several key scenes from the text and an engagement with black feminist thinkers such as Hortense Spillers, I intend to make an argument for the mule as an especially generative site of inquiry and imagination not only in Hurston's oeuvre but in the field of black literary theory more broadly. I seek to illuminate the ways in which a critical engagement with muleness—both as a zoological category with its own fraught history as it pertains to agriculture and subsistence farming in the Americas and as a useful metonym for thinking about the nature of black social life—opens up a number of different avenues through which we might approach *Their Eyes Were Watching God* as a part of Hurston's broader corpus, wherein bestial presence is almost always a narrative element that must be reckoned with. This chapter is intended to reflect the inherent *multiplicity* of muleness as a means of indexing value, as well as to keep track of the indeterminate, uncanny workings of the black feminine in a text that is deeply concerned with how we might read persistence, even abundance, in spaces and, most centrally, onto *forms of human and nonhuman life* that are traditionally marked as nonsites, as vitalized forms of death. It is precisely this critical practice of valuing black and nonhuman life, over and against dominant ways of thinking about or assigning such value, that Hurston wants us to consider when muleness enters the frame.

Whenever Hurston gestures toward the mule, it is a call for us to keep an eye on those that are rendered invisible, whether by force of law or by quotidian social practice. It is the seemingly banal nature of the moments that Hurston draws our attention to, the casualness of the violence deployed against the black women who are treated and discussed as "mules" in the text—as well as the *actual* mules that also make an appearance as these women's metonymic counterparts and fellow targets of men who treat said violence as an explicit means of control or even, oftentimes, recreation—that are of central concern here. Muleness is inextricably linked to this sort of routine violation: the taken-for-granted suffering that occurs beyond the power or purview of social accountability.

Still, this is not all that the figure of the mule makes available to us. Though Hurston certainly returns to the mule repeatedly as a site of unspoken and unspeakable violence, there are also other moments in the novel when it becomes clear that Hurston is interested in the mule as a site of political possibility, of radical imagination set free by misrecognition. Put differently, in addition to functioning as a site of invisibilized suffering and invisibilized labor, the mule also represents a certain kind of *invisibilized interiority,* a black feminist apositionality that bears a striking resemblance to something like freedom in the hold, like fugitivity, like Linda Brent crafting a new life and a new vision from within the loophole of retreat, using the epistolary form to take flight, though she could neither walk nor stand.[1] Thus, when Hurston describes the black woman as the mule of the world, it is clear that this is not only a claim about suffering. For Hurston, muleness is how we might think about black women's kinesthetic and otherwise brilliance in a world bent on their capture. It is how Janie Crawford and the larger ensemble of women she is a part of in this timeless, precious text laugh and lilt and love, knowing they were never meant to survive.[2]

❖

From the first time the mule appears on the scene as a representation of the black feminine, it is abundantly clear that muleness is inextricably linked to a certain recalcitrance, or refusal to be owned, over and against a set of social relations centered on the treatment of black women's every thought, deed, or movement as a form of private property. This relationship between gender and property, between the dominant order and the otherwise possibilities that the mule carries in its wake, is further elaborated on by Janie's grandmother Nanny early on in the novel:

> You know, honey, us colored folks is branches without roots and that makes things come round in queer ways. You in particular. Ah was born back due in slavery so it wasn't for me to fulfill my dreams of whut a woman oughta be and to do. Dat's one of de holdbacks of slavery. But nothing can't stop you from wishin'. You can't beat nobody down so low till you can rob 'em of they will. Ah didn't want to be used for a work-ox and a brood-sow and Ah didn't want mah daughter used dat way neither. It sho wasn't mah will for things to happen lak they did. Ah even hated de way you was born. But, all de same Ah said thank God, Ah got

another chance. Ah wanted to preach a great sermon about colored women sittin' on high, but they wasn't pulpit for me.
Freedom found me wid a baby daughter in mah arms, so Ah said
Ah'd take a broom and a cook-pot and throw up a highway
through de wilderness for her. She would expound what Ah felt.
But somehow she got lost offa de highway and next thing Ah
knowed here you was in de world. So whilst Ah was tendin' you
of nights Ah said Ah'd save de text for you. Ah been waitin' a
long time, Janie, but nothin' Ah been through ain't too much if
you just take a stand on high ground like Ah dreamed.[3]

Here, the figure of the dream appears not as a dream deferred but
as a dream destroyed by material circumstance. That dream, in this
instance, differs from Janie's first dead dream in the novel—
concerned as it was, primarily, with pleasure and autonomy in the
midst of a monogamous love relationship.[4] This is a dream with a
different, though related, set of stakes, a dream of access to the
province of the human in ways that black women have been barred
from historically.

With stunning regularity, Nanny turns to animal figures in
order to give an account of her life experience. Her "dreams of whut
a woman oughta be and to do" are in direct conflict with her being
"used for a work-ox and a brood-sow" by those who claimed legal
ownership over her flesh, her labor, and indeed her very life. Though
the mule is not explicitly invoked in this passage, its haunting presence is nonetheless felt in the language used to describe the daily
experiences of black women living under the conditions of chattel
slavery. There is not only the constant threat of interpersonal violence, both physical and psychic, at the hands of men—as we see
so vividly in Janie's relationships—but an expulsion from the field

of the human subject, the self-possessed agent in control of the functions of one's own body. What appears instead is a vision of life as an invention, a machine, what Marx might call "a speaking implement."[5] For Nanny, the black feminine is a site marred by its relationship to death and quotidian violence, but it is not only that. As she reminds the reader early on, "Nothing can't stop you from wishin'. You can't beat nobody down so low till you can rob 'em of they will."

Though Nanny spends her days in the midst of what many people would call unlivable conditions, she keeps right on wishing, dreaming, sketching out a line of flight. This enactment of the freedom drive is directly linked to the "queer ways" that Nanny describes in the opening lines of the passage.[6] That is, it is exactly the sort of rootlessness that Nanny gives language to, a rootlessness that is also an ongoing, lived critique of patriarchal models of family structure, and kinship broadly construed, which feeds her radical imagination, her meditative tenacity in the face of gratuitous violence. These queer ways are intimately linked to Hortense Spillers's claim in her seminal essay "Mama's Baby, Papa's Maybe: An American Grammar Book" regarding the ways in which the black feminine operates in contrast to, and as a criticism of, normative hierarchies and cartographies of gender:

> But I would make a distinction . . . between "body" and "flesh" and impose that distinction as the central one between captive and liberated subject positions. In that sense, before the "body" there is the "flesh," that zero degree of social conceptualization that does not escape concealment under the brush of discourse or the reflexes of iconography. . . . As Elaine Scarry describes the mechanisms of torture, . . . these lacerations, wounding, fissures,

tears, scars, openings, ruptures, lesions, rendings, and punctures
of the flesh create the distance between what I would designate
a cultural *vestibularity* and the *culture*. . . . This body whose flesh
carries the female and the male to the frontiers of survival bears
in person the marks of a cultural text whose inside has been
turned outside.[7]

Spillers goes on to elaborate on this relationship between captivity,
flesh, and vestibularity, naming the black woman, and the black
feminine in a broader sense, as a locale at which these three terms
intersect with peculiar force:

The flesh is the concentration of "ethnicity" that contemporary
critical discourses neither acknowledge nor discourse away. It is
this "flesh and blood" entity, in the vestibule (or "pre-view") of a
colonized North America, that is essentially rejected from "The
Female Body in Western Culture," but it makes good theory, or
commemorative "herstory" to want to "forget" or have failed to
realize, that the African female subject, under these historic conditions, is not only the target of rape—in one sense, an interior-
ized violation of body and mind—but also the topic of specifically externalized acts of torture and prostration that we imagine
as the peculiar province of male brutality and torture inflicted
by other males. A female body strung from a tree limb, or bleeding
from the breast on any given day of field work because of the
"overseer," standing at the length of a whip, has popped her flesh
open, adds a lexical and living dimension to the narratives of
women in culture and society. This materialized scene of unpro-
tected female flesh—of female flesh "ungendered"—offers a
praxis and a theory, a text for living and for dying, and a method
for reading both through their diverse mediations.[8]

What new possibilities for thinking about the relationship between blackness, gender, and animal life emerge if we take seriously Spillers claim here about both the flesh and what she calls *vestibularity?* How might we reconcile such theorizing with Nanny's own philosophy of race, labor, and gender, in which the very ungendering that Spillers names here is described through the aforementioned invocations of the work-ox and the brood-sow? For Nanny, then, as for Spillers, ungendering is also a transformation *at the level of species;* it is how one is forcibly removed from the province of the human and placed elsewhere.

This violence that both Spillers and Nanny name is what bars the flesh from entering the realm of the body; it is this very availability to such violence and violation that is part of what constitutes the flesh *as such*. And yet the flesh is not only or always a site of terror. It is also, according to Spillers, a site of endless possibility. The flesh, as Elizabeth Grosz reminds us, "supersedes the ontological distinction . . . between the animal and the human."[9] The flesh, in the first instance, is shared and is not inextricably linked to the image of a self-possessed subject that has no need for sociality. Hence, when Spillers invokes the vestibule, positing black flesh as vestibular to what she calls US American "culture," we know that she is also gesturing toward the myriad social possibilities that the flesh makes available to us, possibilities that the body cannot contain or condone.

After all, what is the vestibule if not a space for outsiders? For sinners and latecomers too tired from last night's revelry to rise with the saints? Spiller's invocation of the vestibule is also a call to envision unorthodox forms of social life, to blur the lines between person and thing, human and animal, that the historically marginalized might gather together in the name of a far more compelling project, one more true to the countless, uncanny lives that have never fit within subjectivity's narrow borders. When we take the vestibule seriously as a site for gathering, we are able to read the conflict between Jody and Janie as not only a moment of unethical, interpersonal violence but also an occasion to reckon with what such terror produces and forecloses. Jody's desire to rule Janie, to dominate her and all that she lays her hands to, closes him off to an entire world that Janie has access to, a world in which "flies [are] tumbling and singing, marrying and giving in marriage" and "a dust-bearing bee sink[s] into the sanctum of a bloom; the thousand sister-calyxes arch[ing] to meet the love embrace and the ecstatic shiver of the tree from root to tiniest branch creaming in every blossom and frothing with delight."[10] As Hurston's descriptions of Janie's sense of the natural world throughout the text make clear, Janie's pervasive boredom during her time with Logan or her fear and shame during her time with Jody are not totalizing forces. In spite of and alongside these unrelenting impositions, Janie develops the capacity for ethical relation with other forms of life that are also made subject to the violent whims of men. In this sense, Janie moves through the text as an ecofeminist figure par excellence, one who is always thinking capaciously about the ecological realm and the constellation of affects that it produces.[11] This too is an example of the "insurgent ground" of the female social subject that Spillers references toward the end of her essay.[12] This is what lingering in the vestibule makes possible.

Rather than aspire to domination or control, Janie instead lives into the myriad communal potentialities of the flesh and, in the process, is able to achieve something akin to solidarity with the nonhuman actors all around her:

Take for instance the case of Matt Bonner's yellow mule. They had him up for conversation every day the Lord sent. Most especial if Matt was there himself to listen. Sam and Lige and Walter were the ringleaders of the mule-talkers. The others threw in whatever they could chance upon, but it seemed as if Sam and Lige and Walter could hear and see more about that mule than the whole county put together. All they needed was to see Matt's long spare shape coming down the street and by the time he got to the porch they were ready for him. . . . When the mule was in front of the store, Lum went out and tackled him. The brute jerked up his head, laid back his ears and rushed to the attack. Lum had to run for safety. Five or six more men left the porch and surrounded the fractious beast, goosing him in the sides and making him show his temper. But he had more spirit left than body. He was soon panting and heaving from the effort of spinning his old carcass about. Everybody was having fun at the mule-baiting. All but Janie. She snatched her head away from the spectacle and began muttering to herself. "They oughta beshamed uh theyselves! Teasin' dat poor brute beast lak they is! Done been worked tuh death; done had his disposition ruint wid mistreatment, and now they got tuh finish devilin' 'im tuh death. Wisht Ah had mah way wid 'em all."[13]

What Janie enacts in this scene is a form of interspecies empathy that bears no resemblance to a limited, *self-serving* vision of humaneness but is instead a reckoning with the suffering of non-human beings that demands intercession, if only at the level of desire. Though she cannot act on the mule's behalf in the way that she wants, cannot intercede and enact physical violence against the men tormenting the mule that it might go free, she dares to bear witness, to give voice to what she has seen even if it is only a whisper, a muttering once her head is turned in revulsion. That this is *all she can reasonably do*, that is, speak of the unremitting violence she has witnessed, demands our attention.

What is more, the profound anger Janie expresses toward these men is, all on its own, a radical intervention given prevailing historical and contemporary discourses around the supposed incapacity of black people as it pertains to the love and care of non-human animal lives.[14] What blossoms at the intersection of these two components of the scene—both Janie's overwhelming rage and the quiet protest that, due to her social position, serves as its only reflection in the material world—is a black feminist approach to engaging bestial presence that returns throughout the novel. Though Janie cannot physically lash out here, cannot harm the men the way they are harming the mule or even attempt to gain revenge by taking on the mule's approach to resistant practice—*charging and missing, charging and missing*—she dares to imagine an alternate approach to the organization of human and nonhuman life and eventually gives voice to that imagining. Ultimately, it is this quiet dissent that serves as the condition of possibility for the mule's release. Jody, having overheard Janie without her knowing it, stops laughing when he realizes how she feels about the abuse of Matt Bonner's mule, and he eventually uses his influence to bring the scene to a halt: "Lum, I god, dat's enough! Y'all done had yo' fun now. Stop yo' foolishness and go tell Matt Bonner Ah wants tuh have uh talk wid him right away."[15]

After haggling with Bonner for several minutes, Jody purchases the mule, effectively setting him free to live out his last days without the threat of the yoke or a stranger's fist. During this period, the "free mule," as the townspeople come to refer to him, becomes the subject of all manner of fables, what the narrator refers to as "lies . . . about his free-mule doings."[16] Thus, it is through the social practices of gossip, and *storying*, that the free mule becomes recognizable as a citizen of the town.[17] Through his entry into the forms of orature that the townspeople hold dear, he comes to be granted a personhood not limited to the law or the boundaries of zoological discourse. Through his manumission at the hands of Jody, which was itself the result of Janie Crawford's quiet protestations, the free mule's life comes to represent something other than a citizenship bound to the province of the human and, what is more, a critique of that very category, barred from it as he was only moments before his purchase:

> But way after a while he died. Lum found him under the big tree on his raw bony back with all four feet up in the air. That wasn't natural and it didn't look right, but Sam said it would have been more unnatural for him to have laid down on his side and died like any other beast. He had seen Death coming and had stood his ground and fought it like a natural man. He had fought it to the last breath. Naturally he didn't have time to straighten himself out. Death had to take him like it found him. When the news got around, it was like the end of a war or something like that. Everybody that could knocked off from work to stand around and talk. But finally there was nothing to do but drag him out like all other dead brutes. Drag him out to the edge of the hammock which was far enough off to satisfy sanitary conditions in the town. The rest was up to the buzzards.[18]

The moment the free mule dies, any number of dominant categories are blurred beyond recognition or rescue. Somehow, all at once, the free mule is a "natural man" and a beast and a brute, a prophet that foresees death and a warrior willing to fight it until he can no longer stand. Such multiplicity—that is, the naming of the mule as the nexus of all these divergent figures through which human and nonhuman life is described or else held at bay—is the product of a broader commitment to thinking critically about entanglement, and *interior life*, that permeates the text, a willingness to engage all living things within the world of the novel, both human and nonhuman, as entities that are always already in motion, in process, and thus composed of untold, untapped possibilities. To give an account of the mule's death in the fashion that the townspeople do is to count him as one of their own, to dethrone normative approaches to thinking about the chain of being in favor of an unbounded constellation of affects and assemblages, hierarchy laid low for the sake of relation. That such a decision is made in the wake of the free mule suffering various forms of physical and psychic violence at the hands of Matt Bonner, Lum, and others is of no small consequence.

Here, Hurston is pushing the reader to consider the townspeople's radical imagination as it pertains to the animal's potential for sociality, as well as their all-too-human pettiness. What is evident both in the aftermath of the mule's death and in the novel's opening scene in which the townspeople are described not only as having their bodies "occupied" by brutes but also as having made "burning statements with questions, and killing tools out of laughs"—which for Hurston, I would argue, is a means of describing the lyrical quality of the town gossip and a means of engaging the unabashed meanness that attends such forms of black social life—is that the townspeople are as capable of uncompromising love as they are of unabashed cruelty.[19] The vision of these everyday folks that Hurston provides is one capacious enough to allow for both slander and loving celebration and reflects just the sort of counter-representational ethos that guides the novel and served as the grounds for much of the criticism surrounding it in the moment of its publication.[20]

Muleness, in this passage, operates both as a means of thinking commonality—that is, the experience of black women is akin to that of the actual nonhuman mules that appear in the novel, and that alone serves as the engine of one of the text's guiding metaphors—and as an argument that such proximity, such vestibularity, actually lays the foundation for ethical action beyond what other characters in the scene can fathom or are willing to enact on their own. Janie's willingness to side with the mule, to say *yes* to the call for ethical relation, serves as the condition of possibility for the free mule to become a kind of cult hero, to *simply be left alone*. This letting-be that Janie makes room for allows the free mule to die outside the marketplace and its extractive logic, to die instead among the trees, valiant still, even in defeat. Though he must eventually go where all other brutes go, we understand from Hurston's characterization of nonhuman animals throughout the novel that whatever a brute may be, it is certainly not a symbolic stand-in for emptiness or the absence of will. The brute, for Hurston, is not always a political actor, but it is certainly a social one.[21] Hurston's brute is no subject, nor is it germane to the genre of Man. The brute instead operates as a critique of both these categories simultaneously, unmooring them, unmasking them as hollow positions devoid of fleshly life, what, thinking alongside Spillers, we might imagine as a kind of vestibular proximity: barred from the protections and protocols of Man but adjacent to all other forms of life banned from that blood-stained province. Hurston is clear on the matter. Within the universe of *Their Eyes Were Watching God*, brutes are not socially or otherwise dead.

Thus, when the townspeople claim that death took the free mule like a natural man, it is a radical revision of the Western philosophical tradition's most pervasive ideas about death, a rebuttal to what Martin Heidegger would call the animal's unavailability to death as such, its capacity to "perish" but not die.[22] There are resonances of a counter-Heideggerian critique in other parts of Hurston's corpus, for example, the first line of her famous autobiography *Dust Tracks on a Road*, where Hurston writes, "Like the dead-seeming, cold rocks, I have memories that came out of the material that went to make me. Time and place have had their say."[23] Though one could read this line as merely a gesture toward the physical makeup of rocks as a form of nonhuman, ostensibly inorganic matter—or, put differently, that it is in the very nature of stones to bear the trace of their formational processes, their smoothness or roughness a sign of gradual erosion over time— there is also here, implicitly, the notion that stones possess a mind or some other, radically divergent form of interiority. When Hurston refers to rocks as "dead-seeming," there are not only resonances of performance, that is, *playing* dead, but also an argument about the limits of empiricism. Though the rocks in question might certainly appear to be lifeless, for Hurston, such appearances do not carry the day. In a Heideggerian register, such a claim doubles as an argument that rocks are not without access to the world, which is also to say, without a tether to experience— it is important to note here that Heidegger claims outright in his classic comparison between various forms of organic and inorganic matter that stones and plants are "without world," that animals are "poor-in-the-world," and that humans "have world"—but rather exist on a plane that is largely opaque to human perception.[24] In saying that the free mule dies as a *natural man*, then, Hurston pre-figures Heidegger's argument, shutting it down in advance.

Indeed, over and against Heidegger's vision of nonhuman life as that which is naturally given to a kind of poverty or lack, the townspeople make an argument for the free mule's life as a full life, its death as a meaningful death. Even when they are forced to drag him to the end of the town in order to "satisfy sanitary conditions," there is, surrounding the mule, a mythos that serves to elevate him even in the midst of such inhuman—which of course operates as distinct from, but also in conversation with, *nonhuman*—treatment:

> Out in the swamp they made great ceremony over the mule. They mocked everything human in death. Starks led off with a great eulogy on our departed citizen, our most distinguished citizen and the grief he left behind him, and the people loved the speech. It made him more solid than building the schoolhouse had done. He stood on the distended belly of the mule for a platform and made gestures. When he stepped down, they hoisted Sam up and he talked about the mule as a school teacher first. Then he set his hat like John Pearson and imitated his preaching. He spoke of the joys of mule-heaven to which the dear brother had departed this valley of sorrow; the mule-angels flying around; the miles of green corn and cool water, a pasture of pure bran with a river of molasses running through it; and most glorious of all, No Matt Bonner with plow lines and halters to come in and corrupt. Up there, mule-angels would have people to ride on and from his place beside the glittering

throne, the dear departed brother would look down into hell
and see the devil plowing Matt Bonner all day long in a hell-hot
sun and laying the rawhide to his back. With that the sisters
got mock-happy and shouted and had to be held up by the men-
folks. Everybody enjoyed themselves to the highest and then
finally the mule was left to the already impatient buzzards. They
were holding a great flying-meet way up over the heads of the
mourners and some of the nearby trees were already peopled
with the stoop-shouldered forms.[25]

What does it cost, or create, when the townspeople dare to mock
everything human in death? What is the object and outcome of
such derision? At the free mule's funeral, the townspeople dare to
imagine alternate worlds in which traditional taxonomies are torn
asunder, worlds in which the dominant order of things is inverted
and it is mules, not humans, that lay hold to social and political
power. This scene of communal storying is one of the book's most
resonant instances of black feminist imagination, especially as it
pertains to thinking bestial presence. As was the case in the scene
in which the free mule first appeared, then Matt Bonner's legal
property still, here muleness functions as critical attention to the
presence of nonhuman animals and the singular gravity of their
suffering, as the willingness to imagine a landscape in which those
animals are no longer singular objects of violence and exploitation.
There is a radical philosophy of life being offered by those who de-
liver eulogies at the funeral, but there is also the very matter of
their gathering, this assemblage of black persons daring to assert
not only that the free mule's life was valuable but that he was one
of their own, a citizen. This expansive vision of citizenship is akin
to what Sylvia Wynter refers to as the work of the destruction and

"displacement of the genre of the human of Man."[26] It is vestibular sociality: black social life at the edge.

Still, even in death, there are moments when the free mule is treated as a less-than-human entity, none more vivid perhaps than when his flesh is used as the stage on which his eulogies are read. He is still left to die in the hinterlands, abandoned that the buzzards might take him when they are ready. To be sure, during the final scenes in which the free mule appears, he is not treated as a human might expect to be. One suspects that this is precisely the point. When Hurston claims that the townspeople are mocking everything human in death, included within the scope of that claim are the traditional accoutrements of the death-centered event: the casket, the grave, a church building to house the ceremony. In lieu of such adornment, the free mule's funeral happens outside, all so that he might die where he lived, all so that he might be treated, on this final, social occasion, as an animal—in the sense not of the animal as a site of violence or deprivation but rather of the animal as that which is given to the world, that which flourishes outside the confines of the domestic sphere. This is the crux of the interspecies ethics that Hurston maps out for the reader, a way of *being-alongside* that is not rooted in reductive forms of anthropomorphism but in a desire for interconnection akin to what Édouard Glissant maps out when he writes, "For the poetics of relation assumes that to each is proposed the density (the opacity) of the other. . . . Relation is not a mathematics of rapport but a problematic that is always victorious over threats. To live the relation may very well be to measure its convincing fragility."[27] Following Glissant, then, we might read the scene of the free mule's funeral—as well as his unforeseeable inclusion into the town citizenry only paragraphs earlier—as moments that bear out the sort of fraught exchanges that constitute relation, a collision of opaque actors marked not by smooth collaboration or cohesion but by the collision itself, the very fact of their meeting.

For Glissant, relation is exemplified not by the lifelong bond or the unbreakable phalanx but by strangers screaming in disparate tongues across the void. Relation is found, and freed, in the moments when it is most evasive. Relation is the labor of dragging the free mule to the hinterlands, not only that his body might be given to the earth but also that it might be honored—wept and laughed over. In this sense, the free mule's funeral is the materialized intersection of a black feminist ethic of care and Glissant's vision of "a possible community . . . between mutually liberated opacities, differences, languages."[28] What emerges here, as the finished result of Janie's empathic plea earlier in the chapter, is just such a community, one cohered not by sameness, or even solidarity forged over mutual political interests, but by a liberated opacity bodied forth in everyday acts of stubbornness, foolishness, and joy.

When the townspeople eulogize the free mule, they dare to imagine a fundamentally different world from the one the free mule was made to survive. The vision of mule-heaven rendered here lays low any and all claims to human dominance and superiority and instead offers an eschatology marked by a titanic reversal: the triumph of beast over Man, an order in which justice is meted out against those who once sought to hinder the flourishing of animal lives. That the townspeople include one of their own as the victim of this otherworldly comeuppance—though it is clear at this point in the novel that Matt Bonner is, in no uncertain terms, the least popular man in town—is central to the scene's underlying argument. The very notion of mule-heaven is, at bottom, an acknowledgment of the various ways in which animals are exploited within the culture of the town. It is a paradise complete with amends for the past life, a front-row seat to watch one's former oppressors burn. What is more, there is no need for physical labor in mule-heaven. The resonances between such a vision and the abolitionist eschatology embedded in Negro spirituals such as "I Want to Go Home" is instructive:

> Dere's no rain to wet you
> O, yes I want to go home
> Dere's no sun to burn you
> O, yes I want to go home;
> O, push along, believers, O, yes
> & Dere's no hard trials, O, yes
> & Dere's no whips a-crackin', O, yes
> & My brudder on de wayside, O, yes
> & O, push along, my brudder, O, yes
> & Where dere's no stormy weather, O, yes
> & Dere's no tribulation[29]

What binds "I Want to Go Home" and Hurston's rendering of mule-heaven is not only their otherworldly, utopian sensibilities but also the centrality of freedom from unjust, unpaid labor to those visions. In both instances, heaven functions as heaven precisely because of the absence of the marketplace and the erasure of the unjust labor relations that, in the case of the mule and the sharecropper, the mule and the slave, the mule and the figure of the black, serve as both a primary site of trauma and a constitutive element of their perceived social identity. To craft the image of a universe in which muleness is not inextricably linked to extracted labor or an ongoing availability to violence is to upend the world, to rend the operative terms from the soil in which they were sown.

It is also a purposeful, countercapitalist linking of blackness and muleness, blackness and animality, that runs counter even to other moments in the novel when animals are deployed as a means of illustrating the exploitative conditions of black life lived under the fist of slavery's long *durée*.

Here and elsewhere, Hurston's foremost commitment is not to cleanliness but to murk, to the dirty, difficult labor of giving language to the historically fraught proximity between black flesh and the beasts of the field. Rather than evade this adjacency, Hurston elaborates on it, giving musculature and music to the cut, making a world from what is widely known as nothingness. Even beyond the mule's funeral as an isolated event, the attention to animal worlds made manifest in that moment pervades the text as a whole and provides important insight into Hurston's investment in the mule as a figure that is necessary to think with when we consider the most radical possible vision of black liberation. For Hurston, at least as it pertains to the world of *Their Eyes Were Watching God*, black feminist theorizing is a way of thinking relation, a practice of reading that hinges on one's willingness to pay attention to the flesh—to care for it, even and especially when that flesh is not held precious by the protocols and practices of Man and of the human as it has been historically imagined within the Western philosophical tradition.

Put differently, muleness, as it is deployed not only in the free mule's funeral but indeed in the moments right after, compels us, always, to look where we have not been trained to look:

As soon as the crowd was out of sight they closed in circles. The near ones got nearer and the far ones got near. A circle, a swoop and a hop with spread-out wings. Close in, close in till some of the more hungry or daring perched on the carcass. They wanted to begin, but the Parson wasn't there, so a messenger was sent to the ruler in a tree where he sat. The flock had to wait for the white-headed leader, but it was hard. They jostled each other and pecked at heads in hungry irritation. Some walked up and down the beast from head to tail, tail to head. The Parson sat motionless in a dead pine tree about two miles off. He had scented the matter as quickly as any of the rest, but decorum demanded that he sit oblivious until he was notified. Then he took off with ponderous flight and circled and lowered, circled and lowered until the others danced in joy and hunger at his approach.

He finally lit on the ground and walked around the body to see if it were really dead. Peered into its nose and mouth. Examined it well from end to end and leaped upon it and bowed, and the others danced a response. That being over, he balanced and asked:

"What killed this man?"

The chorus answered, "Bare, bare fat."

"What killed this man?"

"Bare, bare fat."

"What killed this man?"

"Bare, bare fat."

"Who'll stand his funeral?"

"We!!!!!"

"Well, all right now."

So he picked out the eyes in the ceremonial way and the feast went on.[30]

Unlike the townspeople, the buzzards do not necessarily mock everything human in death; rather, they animalize what we might consider to be solely the province of the human. They create their own ceremony around the mule and in doing so refer to him as a man, a man given to death like any other. For the buzzards, the consumption of the dead mule's flesh is both instinct and something other than instinct. There is an order to the proceedings, a decorum that must be acknowledged and adhered to even in this moment of bloody exchange. Hurston turns our attention to the animal world in this scene that we might grasp more fully what she has used the figure of the mule to argue all along, that the animal not only *has a world* but has a world that both encompasses ours and exceeds it, a world that has space for both the funeral and the feasting on the corpse that comes after. In this sense, the buzzards too represent a robust critique of Heidegger's claims about animal experience. Far from worldless, they instead wear the trappings of the (human) world like a garment they can put on and remove at will. They are both in the world and of it; they know its workings well enough to play with its conventions and constraints, precisely *because* of the subjugated position they occupy. For Hurston, the proximity of this scene to the free mule's funeral is also an argument about black humor and the many ways that black social life—by virtue of not only its existence but also its dogged persistence—operates in a similar fashion. Opacity becomes an occasion for analysis, and those who are said to be without an interior grant, once gathered together, the briefest glimpse into the multitudes they contain.

Thus, in this final instance, the mule is again the agent through which we come to understand that animals are as proximate as they are opaque and that it is absurd to assume, as Brian Massumi writes, "that animals do *not* have thought, emotion, desire, creativity, or subjectivity. . . . Is that not to consign animals yet again to the status of automatons?"[31] On this front, Hurston and Massumi have their feet firmly planted on common ground. Up until the final pages of the novel, all of the animal characters in *Their Eyes Were Watching God* live into the kind of historically un-thought affective, intellectual complexity that Massumi gestures toward. Indeed, in the book's closing movement, it is the animals that foretell the hurricane that will spell the end of Janie's rela-tionship with her third and truest beloved, Tea Cake: "Some rab-bits scurried through the quarters going east. Some possums slunk by and their route was definite. One or two at a time, then more. By the time the people left the fields the procession was constant. Snakes, rattlesnakes began to cross the quarters. The men killed a few, but they could not be missed from the crawling horde. People stayed indoors until daylight. Several times during the night Janie heard the snort of big animals like deer. Once the muted voice of a panther. Going east and east."[32] To the end, the animals know beyond knowing. In this respect, they differ greatly from the white residents of the nearby towns, as well as Tea Cake, who claims, in what will prove to be a tragically misplaced moment of trust, "De white folks ain't gone nowhere. Dey oughta know if it's dangerous."[33] Though Janie wants to heed the warning that the animals' collective flight represents, she chooses instead to honor Tea Cake's sense of the situation before them. And though one can certainly understand Tea Cake's logic—that is, that in a socio-political landscape centrally concerned with white safety, keeping tabs on what white folks deem dangerous is always a sound course of action—in the end, it is this reliance on Eurocentric ways of knowing that dooms the pair. Ultimately, Tea Cake will contract rabies from a dog he encounters in the coming flood, and Janie will be forced to shoot him in order to save her own life. That the novel ends on this note, that is, a major death caused by proximity to the animal, is of critical import. From the opening of *Their Eyes Were Watching God*, Hurston makes it clear that there is no communion to be had with the animal without the possibility of death. There is no bond unmarred by blood. This, for Hurston, is the work of the figure of the mule as a problem for thought: how we might collaborate across unfathomable distance and think about difference not as an occasion for domination but as an opportunity to sketch a dying world anew.[34]

4

Dog

_____

Tie Luther B to that cypress. He gon' be alright.
The dog done been rained on before,
he done been here a day or two hisself before,
and we sho' can't take him. Just leave him
some of that Alpo and plenty of water.
Bowls and bowls of water.
We gon' be back home soon this thing pass over.
Luther B gon' watch the place while we gone.
You heard the man—he said Go' and you know
white folks don't warn us 'bout nothing unless
they scared too. We gon' just wait this storm out.
Then we come on back home. Get our dog.

—Patricia Smith, "Won't Be but a Minute"

Fact of the matter is, I trust dogs more than
I trust humans.

—DMX, "Dog Intro"

W hite dogs—which is also to say, dogs that, as a result of those
who claim ownership over their flesh and employ it, exploit
it toward white-supremacist ends that are more or less inextricable

from hegemonic whiteness as a set of sociopolitical protocols and practices—are ubiquitous within the African American literary tradition and beyond. Even a cursory search of the landscape reveals the uncanny reappearance of these particular animal figures time and time again across genre. From Langston Hughes's "Little Dog," a standout in his undertheorized collection of short stories *The Ways of White Folks,* to Carl Phillips's poem "White Dog" to the pack of bloodhounds that bound across the ice after Eliza in *Uncle Tom's Cabin,* there are white dogs everywhere. White dogs that are not only pets but often extensions of the police state, indeed, the very flesh-and-bone entities through which the murderous whims of the police state are made manifest in the everyday lives of those who are property themselves or else the descendants of property, those who own nothing and as such exist as a threat to the logic of private property altogether. Given this implicit doubleness, that is, the historical role of the dog as both dire threat and dearest companion within the bounds of not only black expressive cultures but also the everyday experiences of black folks forced to live at and as the bottommost portion of US racial caste, how might we devise an approach to reading the presence of dogs in African American letters that undermines the cultural mythos and, indeed, the persistent erasure that allows for the common rendering of the figure of the dog as "man's best friend"? Or, along a slightly different vector, what if we were to linger with that particular formulation that we might unsettle it, might bore down into the thinking that gives such a phrase its coherence in order to expose what is at stake in imagining the sort of biologically determined, automatic kinship it implies, a bond between Man and beast ensured and established at the level of species, the dog as an example par excellence of *being-for-the-master* from the very first, enchained the moment it enters the scene?

If the dog is indeed always and already the closest companion of Man, then what happens in a textual moment or social scene in which Man is jettisoned from our line of sight and we find ourselves in worlds, imagined or otherwise, populated by those who live and love at the margins of the genre of Man, those altogether barred from that category and its varied protections? Stated plainly, how might we work toward a theory of black kinship, black friendship *as a way of life*, to borrow the Foucauldian phrasing—by paying close attention to instances throughout literatures of the African diaspora in which black folks and the dogs with whom they share space are able to complicate, and ultimately subvert, the bourgeois sensibilities that give shape and form to any strict, hierarchical relationship between pet and human master-subject.[1] Following Frantz Fanon's formulation that *the black is not a man*, as well as Sylvia Wynter's claim that the work of black feminism is, from one angle, a collective laboring toward *the end of the genre of Man*, I would like to think about what kinship between humans and dogs can look like when that which ostensibly undergirds the identity of the former is something other than domination or sovereign power—that is, when Man is removed from the equation altogether and those who have been historically barred from that very category enter the frame of study. If we can think of human-dog relationships outside a particular, Linnaean vision of species hierarchy and instead embrace a model akin to what Karen Barad and others might call *entanglement*, then what sort of alternative models for thinking sociality across species become available to us?[2] Put differently, if we are willing to militate toward the abolition of the genre of Man and think companionship anew, outside the familiar dialectics that

structure the relationship between pet and master in the first instance, what rises to the fore in the wake? What beauty? What
unthinkable terror?

This chapter will focus primarily on the role of dogs in Jesmyn
Ward's 2011 National Book Award–winning novel *Salvage the
Bones*. Therein, I argue, we are provided with an especially rigorous
foundation for thinking kinship across lines of species via the relationship between the novel's protagonist, Esch; her brother
Skeetah; and China, a white pit bull that doubles as both the family
pet and the primary breadwinner in Esch and Skeetah's home.
Through this doubly defamiliarizing gesture—that is, the posi-
tioning of the female dog as the head of the human household—
as well as others, including the recoding of dogfighting and the
underground spaces in which dogfighting tends to take place, as
sites of both black social possibility and singular human-nonhuman
intimacy, Ward crafts a universe in which dominant taxonomies
are razed to the ground in favor of unruly, unregulated ways of
organizing disparate forms of life. I am interested in lingering with
these moments of indeterminacy toward the end of imagining,
alongside Ward, a more liberating model of interspecies companionship than what is offered within the scope of contemporary animal studies discourse.

By way of opening, I will undertake a close reading of the Carl
Phillips poem "White Dog," in an effort to see what happens when
the immediate threat of violence is removed from a work that contains many of the other elements that have heretofore been discussed as mediating factors in the relationship between black people
and dogs. In the absence of the immediate, looming threat of punishment or violence, how is Phillips able to render his relationship

to the nonhuman? What does the poem teach us about fugitivity and the need for black elsewheres governed by different laws, different grammars of encounter and exchange?

❀

From the first lines of Carl Phillips's "White Dog," the poem provides a working vocabulary for thinking the particularity of the historical relationship between black persons and the dogs they claim as kin and companions, a relationship always already marked by both a reckoning with the utter opacity of the animal other and a willingness to relinquish even a semblance of control or dominion as a direct result of that reckoning:

> First snow—I release her into it—
> I know, released, she won't come back.
> This is different from letting what,
>
> already, we count as lost go. It is nothing
> like that. Also, it is not like wanting to learn what
> losing a thing we love feels like. Oh yes:
>
> I love her.
> Released, she seems for a moment as if
> some part of me that, almost,
>
> I wouldn't mind
> understanding better, is that
> not love? She seems a part of me,
>
> and then she seems entirely like what she is:
> a white dog,
> less white suddenly, against the snow,

who won't come back. I know that; and, knowing it,
I release her. It's as if I release her
because I know.[3]

One is left to wonder what, beyond the briefest insight we are granted here, the poem's speaker *knows*, exactly. That is, what sort of knowledge allows for the loss of the beloved, nonhuman other to serve not as a moment in which one might mourn the loss of property or grieve a dearly departed friend but as an occasion to name the loss as something other than loss, a release that is antecedent, given. The speaker is aware, and says outright in the first stanza, that there is no possibility of reunion or return. Once set free, the white dog will remain free and in remaining free—which is also to say, at a distance beyond the reach of human hands, human gaze, or human control—will destabilize the sort of loyalty or fealty that one readily expects from it, a loyalty that is presumed *at the level of biology*. When the speaker claims that this scene is "nothing like" a moment in which one might let what we "count as lost go," he is, I would like to argue, employing a gesture that can be found throughout African American letters, that is, explicitly naming the difference between letting go of what one had and lost and letting go of what one knows *one did not and never could own*—which is not to say that there is no sense of belonging present in the relationship between the eponymous white dog and the speaker as described here. Instead, "White Dog" models for the reader a vision of belonging without ownership, kinship against the logic of private property.

The speaker does not release the white dog so as to learn something new about grief ("Also, it is not like wanting to learn what / losing a thing we love feels like") or because the depth of his commitment to care for and live alongside her has waned ("Oh yes:/I love her") but rather because the will of the animal flashes before him and demands to be reckoned with as true will, as desire that must be treated ethically, rather than subsumed or repressed in the name of a presumed mastery. Normative relations are forgone altogether here in pursuit of an open relation that accounts for the dog's deep interiority and, what is more, what Jakob von Uexküll would call the animal's relationship to its *umwelt*, its personal life-world, over and against and apart from the speaker's vision of the landscape, his reading of the unstable distinction between the dog and the snow made unstable not only by color but by the unwieldy nature of possession itself.[4] Here, the dog functions as the enfleshment of the wild ostensibly made tame, a subdued, domesticated wildness disappearing into a wildness that can never be curtailed or confined. And for a moment, this wildness is also the wildness of the speaker, a part of himself he "wouldn't mind knowing better."

The speaker thinks to call this impulse love and immediately thinks better of it. The gesture toward the elevation of the human emotional life against, even *through*, the flesh of the white dog is instead made into an object of critique. Rather than understanding the dog as a technology through which the speaker might come to a higher plane of self-understanding or otherwise arrive at an epiphany about his interior world that depends on the dog in an abstract sense but could just as easily be projected onto another nearby, nonhuman actor, the speaker opts for a vision of love— which in the Phillips poem we might also read as a particularly black love that blurs the space between entanglement and relation, indeed that dances in the chaos produced by the caesura that might have separated the two terms in the first instance—that rejects solipsistic introspection or dominion in favor of things unknowable, things unseen. Though the speaker may feel as if the white dog is *a part of him*—which is distinct from a mutual entanglement and registers instead as a rendering of the animal-as-extension—and indeed experience her companionship this way in the course of their shared, quotidian experience, there is nonetheless the fact of her *dogness*, a fact that returns throughout the poem to complicate and ultimately unmoor that feeling, throwing it into relief in the wake of the storm that doubles as the occasion of the dog's refusal of such a fiction, her preference for what lies beyond the bounds of the domestic sphere. The dog's "release," then, works in a double sense. Her freedom is bound up with the will of the speaker but is not reducible to it. The speaker releases the dog once it becomes clear that she is *already free of him*, that she has always had her own set of concerns, her own *bauplan*, or "building plan," in Uexkül-lian terms, her own understanding of the "meaning carriers and meaning-factors" in the lived environment.[5] The speaker merely recognizes this desire and chooses to honor it rather than repudiate its pull. It is the thinking that undergirds this choice, that is, the critical interpretative leap from *seems* to *is* that marks the transition from the poem's fourth stanza to its fifth, that is our central concern: "and then she seems entirely like what she is / a white dog, / less white suddenly, against the snow, / who won't come back. / I know that; and, knowing it, / I release her. It's as if I release her / *because* I know." At the close of the poem, we are given an image of dogly affect, of *dogness*, that serves as something of a discursive intervention. For Phillips, the white dog is legible as such not because of her presumed desire for a human master but rather the converse. It is the dog's very distance from the whims and inner workings of the human that mark her position. What

Phillips uncovers here is a decidedly asymmetrical desire, a human need for companionship marked by proximity, and often obedience, that does not originate with the dog but emerges here as a product of a particular kind of androcentrist cosmology. The white dog herein refuses to live as a reflection of a man's inner world and instead asserts her own, daring to relinquish her particularity (less white suddenly, against the snow) that she might enter the clearing, indulge in its endless possibility.

To be sure, the *letting go* we see modeled in Phillips's "White Dog"—a move that, it bears mentioning, is in the first instance an ethics, a necessary reckoning with the reality of material and otherwise worlds that exist beyond the province of human knowledge—is a mode of planetary thinking. It is a form of black sociality that asserts that "what love and connection the speaker holds for and with [the white dog] must be held with the knowledge that she is her own completely separate entity, free to remove herself from the speaker entirely, and not subject to human emotions."[6] The speaker's willingness to critique a vision of human love that seeks to oversimplify the sheer breadth and capacity of the dog's life-world—which is also to say, a love that effectively imagines nonhuman animals as nonentities without interior lives worth considering—is also an unsettling of the very terms by which many people have come to understand dogs as a distinct category of animal life:

> It does not do any good composing sonnets if you are a dodo. You are obviously missing the intelligence you need to survive (in the dodo's case, this was learning to avoid new predators such as hungry sailors). With this as our starting point, the dog is arguably the most successful animal on the planet, besides us. Dogs

have spread to all corners of the world, including inside our homes, and in some cases onto our beds. While the majority of mammals on the planet have seen a steep decline in their populations as a result of human activity, there have never been more dogs on the planet than there are today. . . . I am fascinated with the kind of intelligence that has allowed dogs to be so successful. Whatever it is—this must be their genius.[7]

For Vanessa Woods and Brian Hare, the genius of dogs is inextricable from what we might read as an unsurpassed ability to adapt to the ways of the dominant species, to move with and alongside humankind in a way that makes their presence invaluable. What remains altogether unchallenged in this vision of evolutionary history, however, and disturbingly so, is the sleight of hand that allows for the wanton destruction of nonhuman life all over the planet to enter the frame as mere "human activity." What lingers behind such phrasing are too many dead bodies to count, entire ecosystems reduced to cinders in the name of human progress and the advancement of Western civilization. Further, to argue that dogs have only fared as well as they have over the centuries because of their usefulness to the human project as living actors rather than as primarily food or fuel, that they have flourished, at least at the level of population, because of what is posited here as some sort of organic inclination toward *servility*, is to also damn the wild, to pathologize the myriad forms of plant and animal life that have and continue to buck against human domination in ways that are and are not legible within the bounds of an anthropocentrist worldview. Further, what persists throughout this passage, though it remains largely unmarked, unacknowledged, or else repressed, is the capacity of the dog to *lie*, to live in the home or lie in the bed of a human master simply as a means to its own unknowable ends. How might the worldview presented by Woods and Hare be complicated by a reading of the dog as a double agent or quiet insurgent, the dog not as an extension of a human master but an infinitely more complex being, one with a set of desires that are largely unknowable to the human mind? In this regard, the Phillips poem serves as a useful counterpoint to the sort of widely accepted thinking about not only the long-standing social role but also the ostensibly hard-set neurological predispositions of dogs. Phillips's is a vision of dog life without any masters worthy of the title, one in which the *bauplan* of his companion animal takes precedence over the world he once imagined for them both.

From the opening scenes of *Salvage the Bones,* it is clear the novel is one that will require readers to recalibrate and revise our most basic categories, to seek out fresh, more nuanced vocabularies for the social and psychic world unfolding before us. The story begins with a white dog gone feral, legibly unsettled, at least, seemingly uncontrollable: "China's turned on herself. If I didn't know, I would think she was trying to eat her paws. I would think that she was crazy. Which she is, in a way. Won't let nobody touch her but Skeet. When she was a big headed pit bull puppy, she stole all the shoes in the house, all our black tennis shoes Mama bought because they hide dirt and hold up until they're beaten soft. . . . Now China is giving like she once took away, bestowing where she once stole. She is birthing puppies."[8] From this opening scene, then, we already have a sense of some of the major themes that will serve to structure the novel. Everywhere we find the language of conflict and collision: the dog, China, *turning on herself,* the image of the

black shoes beaten soft by use, the birth of a litter of puppies as a
kind of compensatory gesture in the wake of a long-standing debt.
The first glimpse we get into the psychic life of the text's narrator
betrays an eye for metaphor and violence alike, a keen attention to
the way categories fold onto and over one another and never without
the potential for loss. Motherhood is the opening scene's central
object of concern, and it is absolutely essential that there is more
than one mother present when the narrative begins—in no small
part because what Ward provides readers with here is an alternative language for motherhood. To become a mother, Ward seems
to say, is also always, in some sense, *to go crazy,* to lose the sense of
oneself as a single being and enter into a kind of embodied multiplicity that challenges the dominant vision of an enclosed, self-
contained subjecthood. For China to become a mother, she must
lose herself, implode, and somehow simultaneously make right the
damage she does when she first enters the world. Motherhood, as
it is described here, is inextricable from the proliferation of brute
force, chaos deployed in all directions. And this destruction is not
at all separate from the in-breaking of life into the world but constitutive of it. There is no new birth without destruction, no life
without a certain version of the world coming to a close: "China is
licking the puppies. I've never seen her so gentle. I don't know what
I thought she would do once she had them: sit on them and smother
them maybe. Bite them. Turn their skulls to bits of bone and blood.
But she doesn't do any of that. Instead she stands over them, her
on the side and Skeetah on the other like a pair of proud parents,
and she licks."[9] What becomes clear not long after this passage is
that China is a fighter, Skeetah her coach and trainer and kin, the
pair of them a force to be reckoned with in the dogfights that
reign as a popular pastime in the novel's primary setting of Bois

Sauvage, Mississippi. *Bois Sauvage* is, of course, French for "wild wood," and it is this motif of wildness, the constant presence of actors sentient and otherwise that cannot or will not be tamed or made civil, that takes center stage throughout the text. Thinking with the terms that the novel's narrator, Esch, makes readily available for us, we can immediately read a linkage between the "craziness" she attributes to China and a descent from domestication into a certain wildness, a line of flight taken away from the sort of discipline that has made China such a dominant force within Bois Sauvage's community of animal prizefighters. It is China's very identity as a fighter, however, that complicates her newfound role as a mother and caretaker for Esch. What she expects the moment the puppies come into the world is not anything legible as love or affection but instead the kind of violence for which China is best known, a kind of unrelenting cruelty that doubles as the condition of possibility for Esch and the rest of her family to continue to live.

At the moment readers arrive in the world of *Salvage the Bones*, it is China, the companion animal and new mother, that has served as the breadwinner in Esch's household for some time, a role she entered, we are led to believe, once Esch and Skeetah's father stops working in the wake of their own mother's unexpected death. Thus, when Esch describes Skeetah standing with China as if the two are "a pair of proud parents," there is also a gesture, I think, toward the sort of antinormative, distinctly *wild* kinship relations that have emerged in the wake of the loss of the potential for a nuclear family, the alternative possibilities that have opened up given the absence of the mother who preceded China, the woman whom we are never introduced to, in fact, by any name other than "Mama." It is not only the present violence of motherhood, then, that haunts the novel but also the ghost of a mother lost, a mother who never got the chance to raise the youngest of the children in the house, Randall and Junior, and only saw the narrator, Esch, grow to be a young girl.

Mama's absence is felt everywhere. The wildness we see from Esch and others is intended, in part, to be a reflection of their ostensible lack of adult guidance, what happens when the ones left in charge of the house are a teenage boy and his dog. To Ward's credit, this aspect of the text never transforms into a kind of cautionary tale. Quite the contrary. Though Mama's absence is clearly the source of all sorts of interpersonal conflict and individual trauma that we see characters wrestling with throughout the novel, the difficulty of reckoning with her ghost also serves as the foundation for Esch's connection with China, her understanding of the dog not only as a family pet but as a comrade in a meaningful sense: "Color washes across the stick like a curtain of rain. Seconds later, there are two lines, one in each box. They are skinny twins. I look at the stick, remembering what it said on the packaging in the store. Two lines means that you are pregnant. You are pregnant. I am pregnant. I sit up and curl over my knees, rub my eyes against my kneecaps. The terrible truth of what I am flares like a dry fall fire in my stomach, eating all the fallen pine needles. There is something there."[10] Esch's description of her pregnancy as a "terrible truth" is especially pointed here given its proximity to her description of China's experience giving birth. The fear she feels is clearly not only that of the potential presence of a child, and thus also an entire vision of the future she did not imagine or plan for, but also what registers as a fear of becoming what she has borne witness to, an animal gone mad, a subject without a center or stable ground to rely on. And it is this fear of losing control, of being given over to wildness, that pursues Esch constantly. It manifests itself primarily as a kind of recurring, inverted personification at the level of description, entire taxonomic categories stretching until they go slack, slipping into one another, forming new assemblages. When describing a lover, Esch claims that "his muscles jabbered like chickens."[11] At one point, she refers to her childhood home as a "drying animal skeleton, everything inside . . . was evidence of living salvaged over the years."[12] In the landscape that Esch paints for us, there is a porousness between worlds, a kinship and commonality among living and nonliving things alike. Following Colin Dayan's claim that "dogs stand in for a bridge—the bridge that joins persons to things, life to death, both in our nightmares and in our daily lives," I wonder if we can think about Esch and China's relationship as just this sort of forged connectivity across the boundary of species, a rapport beyond blood that also extends to the vast majority of person-nonperson relations that compose their shared social world.[13] What Dayan calls a bridge is also a blurring, a marring of distinctions rooted in white-supremacist anthropocentrism. For Esch already knows that there is an antecedent, forced proximity between her and China long before she discovers that she is pregnant, knows that they are both considered—at least, under the terms of civil society's flattening optics—what I would like to think of here as *low life*. China, after all, is not only a dog but also a pit bull and thus always already criminalized in advance by virtue of pervasive social stigma. And she is not only a pit bull but also a fighting dog, a double outlaw. Esch is a poor, dark-skinned black girl from a town in the Deep South that is named outright for its utter lack of civility, its murky depths and untamed flora. What emerges from this shared exclusion from the realm of the proper is, I think, the possibility of an altogether distinct relationship to the category of ownership itself, a robust, working vocabulary through which we might imagine the abolition of species hierarchy. To think with and about *low life* in its many registers is to turn a critical eye toward the sites and non-subjects that have historically been considered unworthy of study. It is to take seriously the myriad social protocols and practices that flourish at the level below which one cannot go, to immerse oneself in the infinite possibilities dreamt up and given flesh by the kids and beasts and broken things that have made a way out of no way, that have forged a kind of life underground, in the blackness at the bottom of the world.

   To be clear, the putative *lowness* of low life is not rooted in a moralist viewpoint, though it is certainly a gesture toward the judicial, nor is it necessarily a description of the inherent quality of the lives of those who might be said to inhabit such a category. Instead, the phrase is intended to operate as an ongoing critique and complication of life in the upper divisions of mainstream social strata—what Lauren Berlant and others might call *the good life*—and what is more, as a spatial description of an elsewhere in which the forms of life that are repressed, subjugated, and every day subdued might have room to establish a robust sociality among themselves, a commons even outside the commons, below it.[14] This is the world into which Esch enters when she discovers that she is pregnant and becomes part of the larger community of mothers, human, nonhuman, and otherwise that serve as the central focus of *Salvage the Bones*. Dayan writes,

> How can I seize on dog life in words? Dogs live on the track between the mental and the physical and sometimes seem to tease out a near-mystical disintegration of the bounds between them.

What would it mean to become more like a dog? How might we come up against life as a sensory but not sensible experience? We all experience our dogs' unprecedented and peculiar attentiveness. It comes across as an exuberance borne by a full heart. . . . What does it mean to think outside our selves and with other beings? For dogs, thought is immersed in matter. Not sympathy or sentiment but something more acute and unsettling. When dogs find themselves in the wrong place at the wrong time, belonging to the wrong kinds of people or protecting earnestly the homes of their human companions, they gather themselves up in their flesh, and in a state of prescience and acceptance, they prepare for the time when life stops, as they slip away toward stillness. It is not that they do not know what is going to happen to them but that they know too well.[15]

Dayan's description of what we might effectively think of as a kind of *becoming-alongside* is immensely useful as it pertains to sketching a fuller picture of the way Esch describes her own internal universe, one in which she is constantly finding herself connected to China by both ineluctable violence and tenacious love. It is this bond that compels Esch to move from the strictly sensible into the *sensory,* to gather herself up in her flesh and enter a much more complicated, often more dangerous, relationship with the broader social world. At several points, China's fearlessness becomes Esch's. Indeed, it becomes clear that the sort of unquenchable, inviolable fierceness that drives China as a fighter is altogether inextricable from the way we see Esch move throughout the social milieu of Bois Sauvage. One gets the sense that Esch *feels everything,* that there is no detail of the lived environment—or the inner lives of her fellow characters—that is not readily available to her capacious vision, her razor wit. Esch is quiet, yes, but there is always a tempest lurking beyond the veil, a rage repressed but never quenched. This willingness to engage with a black girl's fury—this anger that is nothing if not the desire to live over and against a psychic and political order sharply oriented against the expression or cultivation of such desire—and to render it as a sign of resistance rather than a mark of pathology or dysfunction, is part of what distinguishes *Salvage the Bones* as a text of great importance for the way we might work toward a theory of black feeling. In this theory, we might return to the wild as a means through which to abolish the stranglehold of a white-supremacist imaginary—wherein, it bears noting, a vision of civility is championed that is always already contradictory in the first instance given the history and present effects of settler colonialism—turning antiblack pathology on its head via a refusal that is also a critical embrace, a recoding of terms that makes the space of the beast, the animal, the savage, or the barely salvaged a space that we might inhabit with joy. Here is where we see in action a working lexicon for sociality outside the bounds of the civil, how everyday people live and die at the underside of modernity.

Thus, the connection between China and Esch is made manifest not only in slippages between the human and nonhuman realm at the level of description, or in the ways in which both help us to reimagine the distinction between tenderness and aggression, but also in the individual relationships between China, Esch, and their respective sexual partners: Manny and Kilo. In a scene that serves as a critical point of insight into the gender politics of the novel—which is also to say, the various ways in which species hierarchy enters the world of the text *by another name*—we are granted access into both Manny's own, deeply sexist ways of thinking about

the relationship between sex and strength and a compelling counterpoint from Skeetah: "'Any dog that give birth like that is less
strong after. Even if you don't think it. Price of being female.'
Finally Manny glances at me. It slides over me like I'm glass.
Skeetah laughs. It sounds as if it's hacking its way out of him. 'You
serious? That's when they come into they strength. They got something to protect.' He glances at me, too, but I feel it even after he
looks away. 'That's power.'"[16] In opposition to Manny's absurd,
cruel schema, Skeetah argues here that motherhood is the site
of a kind of strength that—unlike a legibly patriarchal form of
power—is given charge not by the freedom to dominate land or
women or labor but rather by *the call of the other,* the call to relation. It is the arrival of the child in the world that inaugurates this
singular strength, this strength that is so often called, as Manny
makes plain, weakness or loss. Skeetah's reversal, his marking of
the figure of the mother as also the site of a strength that cannot
be readily accessed otherwise, cannot be tapped outside of the
mother-child bond, is a moment of refusal that doubles as an occasion in which Ward is showing us how to read the novel, how to
trace the thread of the mother as both protector and agent of wide-
scale destruction. For Ward, the *coming into strength* that Skeetah
invokes often carries with it tremendous consequences, the proliferation of unexpected casualties, bodies left broken in the wake of
a mother's rage.

Though this idea is most readily visible as it pertains to the personification of Hurricane Katrina toward the novel's conclusion,
it becomes clear at various points that China too is more often than
not operating from a position in which her reasons for deploying
certain kinds of hostility, though they might be explicable to
readers, certainly do not read according to any neat anthropomor-

phism that might endear us to China as a character. There is a pair of scenes, for instance, in which she attacks her own puppies. Though the first, Skeetah explains, is a moment in which China is trying to keep the rest of her litter safe from one of their siblings that has been infected with parvovirus, the second moment, in which she mauls the puppy that most clearly resembles his father, Kilo, remains more or less opaque. Skeetah states it plainly, even throwing in a bit of rhyme for emphasis: "We savages up here on the Pit. Even the gnats. Mosquitoes so big they look like bats."[17] This moment of self-naming, this critical embrace of *savagery*, is one of the novel's greatest gifts. In Bois Sauvage, and in the Pit in particular, where China fights and trains and eventually gives birth, there is a relationship to and with violence that has absolutely no truck with the language of civil society. Savagery is the way of the Pit, and that not only means that certain forms of violence are permissible but also that this thing called violence is blurred, transformed, and ultimately reflected in the world of Bois Sauvage in ways that structure the intimate relationships between the text's central characters. There is no place in the text untouched by the brutality that surrounds this community, the violence that shapes everyday life at the world's bladed edge.

Manny's cruelty to Esch in particular is a regular point of reference throughout the novel, and it is the combination of this unerring meanness and his direct, ongoing, and unfounded criticism of China that establishes a clear parallelism between him and Esch on one end of the analogy and China and Kilo on the other:

Rico is Manny's cousin, the boy from Germaine who bought his dog, Kilo to mate with China. Rico's big red muscle of a dog with a killing jaw. It was Manny who talked up Kilo to Skeetah. . . .

> Manny would talk shit whenever we were all out under the trees
> as if he could lessen the wonder of Skeetah's prized dog. He
> thought he could dim her, that he could convince us she wasn't
> white and beautiful and gorgeous as a magnolia on the trash-
> strewn hardscrabble Pit, where everything else is starving,
> fighting, struggling. . . . When they mated, China had let Kilo
> lick her from behind, let him mount. Smiled like she liked it. . . .
> Kilo had placed his big mouth on her neck like he was kissing
> her and slobbered on her. She'd snapped at him, figured it for a
> hold. Hated the submission of it. She nicked him, snapped at him
> until she threw him off. She'd drawn blood, he hadn't.[18]

Ward's depiction of the moment in which Kilo and China encounter each other lays bare the inherent, myriad violences that
produce the plot's point of origin, the terror that serves as the condition of possibility for China to become a mother. We are not
spared a detail. We find out that Kilo's "killing jaw" was, in some
sense, a selling point—that, of course, and China's notorious
hunger for blood beyond even the demands of competition, a fury
well known throughout the dogfighting circuit that she and
Skeetah ran through in the moments leading up to this one. And
yet it is something more than bloodlust that we are compelled to
see in this scene, something more even than the muscle memory
that Esch alludes to toward the close of the passage. China's refusal to heel or be held by anyone except for Skeetah is a reflection
of their particular bond, one that exceeds mastery or metonymy.
For China is indeed a part of Skeetah, as she is a part of Esch,
though in ways that complicate any easy, straightforward vision of
human dominion or doggish servility. Given Skeetah's earlier definition of what makes the denizens of the Pit especially "savage,"

we know that it is a designation that travels across species—even the gnats and mosquitoes are larger than life, mutated beyond clear taxonomic boundary. It is apparent that we are meant to read China as not so different from Skeetah or Big Henry or Randall or Junior or even Esch with regard to her everyday experiences of violence and intimacy as twin edges of the same blade.

The primary distinction that emerges to mark China is the shimmering whiteness of her fur, and even this is thrown into relief, in a sense, by the other descriptions of her that abound throughout the book. Put differently, as a result of her position as a white dog that is *blackened by her breed*—and here, I am indebted to the work of not only Dayan but popular writers such as Malcolm Gladwell who have written publicly about the ways in which pit bulls have become the objects of state repression as a result of their association with poor, largely nonwhite US American populations—but also her place within a larger kinship network made up almost entirely of poor black folks, we are compelled to rethink the metonymic labor of whiteness in the text, to consider the other ways in which China's whiteness might be working at the level of device.[19] Her name is a fitting a place to begin. Though there is the surface reading that draws a one-to-one connection between the whiteness of China's fur and the whiteness of a set of fine china dishes and stops there, there are also any number of other readings available given the various ways that China is characterized by Esch, as well as the specific scenarios in which her phenotypical whiteness is mentioned. Keeping with the coupling of China the dog and *fine china*, we can perhaps read her name in the first instance as a gesture toward delicacy or refinement, gentility over and against the harsh surroundings from which Skeetah and Esch have emerged. To come from Bois Sauvage, to live and work in the Pit and yet still name one's dog China, is to assert a certain kind of beauty where there is said to be none, a savage beauty that is not as easily break-able as fine china, though it may bear its trace.

In this vein, we might also read the name *China* as a marker of smoothness, a testament to the way she moves in every fight, fur and skin so smooth that no other dog can touch her, much less get a hold going that will do any real damage. To be china is to be precious, well kept and cared for. And it is in this register that I think we find the most interesting component of China's name at the symbolic level, that is, the mutual adoration between her and Skeetah. Skeetah does not refer to himself nor is he referred to as her owner but regularly mentions her as his teammate and collab-orator, the nonhuman companion he cherishes and trains along-side: "I wonder if he has trained her to do this, to stand at his side, to not dirty even her haunches with sitting so that they gleam. China is white as the sand that will become a pearl, Skeetah is black as an oyster, but they stand as one before these boys who do not know what it means to love a dog the way that Skeetah does."[20] The love that Esch invokes here is one that destabilizes kind and kin and color in one fell swoop: Skeetah's dark oyster and China's ashen pearl are rendered almost indistinguishable by the smooth blur of their relation. China's whiteness is representative, I think, of both what Jacques Derrida might call "the infinite distance of the other" and a Motenian vision of blackness in which blackness "claims" those who are not necessarily legible as members of the African diaspora—or even and especially, I would argue, the cat-egory of the human—but nonetheless are marked and marred by their condemnable proximity to black people, black locales.[21] China is an example of the ways in which blackness destabilizes the very practice of taxonomic distinction, a dog that is *optically* white but undoubtedly blackened as a result of her daily participation in black social and public life, as well as her ongoing companionship with Skeetah. Her chromatic whiteness functions, then, we might imagine, not as a corollary to racial whiteness but along an altogether different symbolic vector. When Esch compares China to a magnolia blossom or sand, it is an attempt to insert her into a broader ecopoetics that asserts vitality where it is not readily visible, to praise the starkness of her bright white coat the way one might praise a star, only visible against the blackness that serves as its condition of perceptibility. Indeed, when one pivots from Esch's description of China's chromatic whiteness to Skeetah's—and this is no small matter in part because we are led to assume that it is Skeetah who named China in the first place—during the course of a fight, we arrive at a rather striking litany of descriptors, none of which reinscribe what we might think of as a color theory delimited by the restrictions of a white-supremacist imaginary: "*China White,* he breathes, *my China. Like bleach, China, hitting and turning them red and white, China. Like coca, China, so hard they breathe you up and they nose bleed, China. Make them runny, China, make them insides outsides, China, make them think they snorted the razor, China. Leave them shaking, China, make them love you, China, make them need you, China, make them know even though they want to they can't live without you, China, My China,* he mumbles, *make them know, make them know, make them know.*"[22] China's name and her color by extension seem to signify a distinctly *low* sensibility and set of affects: intoxication, addiction, indiscernibility. China is a force that obscures, rearranging every border and boundary, blurring inside and outside, pleasure and pain, life and death. And it is this indeterminacy, bodied forth in the form of a song crafted by her closest companion, that gives charge to

China's color as a useful metonym for thinking outside what we might normally ascribe to whiteness. Here, rather than imagining her coat in contrast to the wildness of Bois Sauvage, the irreducible, irredeemable blackness of its inhabitants and all that they touch, we can instead read China's whiteness as a site of intoxication and excess, her whiteness as always already blackened, as a "dark white" even, to use Samuel Beckett's phrasing.[23] Through China's flesh and the proximity to blackness she enacts in her everyday movement throughout the world of the Pit and beyond, whiteness and blackness as semiotic markers are muddled, thrown into flux. China must *make them know* who she is, make them know her strength, her ferocity and skill, because of the supposed distance between what her flesh signifies and the world she inhabits, the shine of her coat and the dirt and grime from which she emerges.

In truth, it is the dirt and the grime that creates the bond beyond blood that sutures Kilo and China and Esch and Manny, this spatial and otherwise proximity that tethers their futures together—and not only their futures, we come to find, but all those who choose the life that Skeetah and China have chosen, life *at the edge of the life*, to use Dayan's term, sociality beyond the borders of the civil:

> They will all match today, one dog against another. The boys have been drawn by gossip of the fight between Kilo and Boss to the clearing like the Argonauts were to Jason at the start of his adventure. They will throw their own dogs into the ring, each hoping for a good fight, a savage heart, a win, to return home from the woods, their own dangerous Aegean Sea, to be able to say, *My bitch did it* or *My nigga got him*. Some of the boys are ner-

vous; they put their hands in their pockets, take them out, swing
their sweat rags in the air and swat at gnats. Some of the boys
are confident: shoulders round and grinning. . . . A hawk circles
in the air above us, turns, vanishes.[24]

Here, in the clearing, the unrelenting forms of restriction that
govern the lives of these boys are altogether cast aside, eschewed
in favor of a worldview wherein the boundaries between forms of
life come crashing down. Again, the *savage* appears not as a marker
of derision or worthlessness but as a modality defined by courage
and tenacity. The savage heart is that which flourishes in the midst
of the unlivable, which persists over and against an entire structure set up against it from the very start. In what constitutes one
of the book's essential turns, we come to see that the violence to
which these boys expose their companion animals is the same violence they experience every day. Again, it is the commonplace
nature of this brutality—not only its frequency *but that it is held in
common*—that makes all the difference. This is a violence that extends even beyond the human-dog relationships in the novel as
structured within the bounds of the fight and into language that
serves as the condition of emergence for what we might think of,
following Giorgio Agamben, as *relation without rank*.[25] In such a
space, Esch's repetition of *my bitch did it* and *my nigga got him* is a
clear instance not only of a certain kind of black vernacular
repurposing—wherein phrases traditionally used as gendered and
racialized epithets become terms of both endearment and empowerment—but also of a desire to think kinship across the human
and animal realms rooted in familiarity and a sense of pride. Such
reversals are commonplace throughout *Salvage the Bones* and reflect Ward's commitment to creating a narrative landscape in

which no categories remain stagnant or pure. Everything here is on the move; everything warps and loses its mooring.

The big fight that the boys have gathered to see is between Kilo and Boss, but it is the final fight of the novel, a match between Kilo and China, that ends up taking up more real estate than any other in the text, an exchange that ends in the only moment of internal dialogue we get from any of the animal characters:

> She is fire. China flings her head back into the air as if eating oxygen, gaining strength, and burns back down to Kilo and takes his neck in her teeth. She bears down, curling to him, a loving flame, and licks. She flips over and is on top of him, even though he still has her shoulder. He roils beneath her. She chews. Fire evaporates water. *Make them know make them know make them know they can't live without you,* Skeetah says. China hears. *Hello, father,* she says, tonguing Kilo. *I don't have milk for you.* China blazes. Kilo snaps at her breast again, but she shoulders him away. *But I do have this.* Her jaw is a mousetrap snapped shut around the mouse of Kilo's neck.[26]

Skeetah's chant appears to us anew here, given fresh life by China's tenacity. In this final fight, the knowledge that China offers to all those who are looking on is also a kind of counterknowledge, an infusing of the sign of the mother with a certain destructive force and brute strength. In the small piece of internal monologue we bear witness to, she addresses Kilo as *father* in a way that signals everything but kinship and actually serves to distance him as an object of empathy or affection. Kilo's relationship to China extends only as far as his contribution of genetic material—the traits for which he was selected as a breeding partner—and goes no further. She has no milk for him, no compassion or care—only fire, only the strength of her neck and the cut of her white teeth. This image of the figure of the mother as a source of great terror, indeed, the mother as destroyer or unstoppable force, is not limited to China. By the novel's end, when Hurricane Katrina has ravaged the land and there is barely a home standing in Bois Sauvage, Esch will refer to the storm not only as "the mother that swept into the Gulf and slaughtered" but also, later on, as "the murderous mother who cut us to the bone but left us alive, left us naked and bewildered as wrinkled newborn babies, as blind puppies, as sun-starved newly hatched baby snakes" and, finally, as "the mother we will remember until the next mother with large, merciless hands, committed to blood, comes."[27] In *Salvage the Bones*, motherhood is a category that is open to both the nonhuman and the *nonliving*. Esch's aforementioned mother, who, again, is referred to only as "Mama" throughout the text, appears primarily as a phantom, never speaking, animate only in the brief flashbacks that Esch provides.

Nonetheless, it is this constellation of mothers—Katrina, Mama, China, and Esch—each inhabiting a different position in a normative hierarchy of biological life, that teaches us how to read *Salvage the Bones* for signs of joy and vitality, where some might see only blight, a great land laid to waste. For it is in the wake of Katrina's great destruction, when the debris has smashed its collective head into the homes of the dispossessed, countless shards of glass glinting like dewdrops against the dead wet earth, that we encounter a truly breathtaking moment of black sociality somehow breaking through: "Christophe and Joshua's porch was missing, and part of their roof. A tree had smashed into Mudda Ma'am and Tilda's house. And just as the houses clustered, there were people in the street, barefoot, half naked, walking around felled trees, crumpled trampolines, talking with each other, shaking their heads, repeating one word over and over again: *alive alive alive alive.*"[28] Even after the end of the world, then, we find that there is still an occasion for gathering. Over and against a philosophy of bare life or social and civic death that might name these men and women and children and animals already long gone, there is a refusal bodied forth in the very act of speaking one to another, of returning repeatedly to that which is supposedly farthest from their reach: a life worth recognizing as such. The Katrina survivors of Bois Sauvage go as far as to turn their refusal to die into a kind of spell, a song that speaks life where it simply cannot be, futurity where all available metrics signal finitude. Just as Esch calls us to see China as her sister in the novel's final pages, the black poor of Bois Sauvage demand that we think of life and death, abundance and utter lack, not as clearly demarcated antipodes but as altogether inextricable.[29] Death, to invert the Nietzschean formulation, *is a species of life.*[30] For the denizens of the Pit—not unlike those who inhabit the Muck, the Clearing, the Bottom, and countless other spaces in and through which the historically marginalized have forged imposed nothingness into a kind of living—there is a flourishing that exceeds the reach and restrictions of modernity.[31] There is a world beneath the world. And it shimmers.

5

Shark

I have sometimes, not without horrour, seen the dismal Ra-
paciousness of these Animals; four or five of them together
shoot to the bottom under the Ship to tear the dead Corps
to pieces, at each bite an Arm, a Leg, or the Head is snapt
off; and before you can tell twenty have sometimes divided
the Body amongst them so nicely that not the least Particle
is left.

—William Bosman, *A New and Accurate Description of
the Coast of Guinea* (1705)

I come to this place, . . . to this water that was bigger than the
whole world. And I looked out, . . . and I seen these bones rise
up out of the water. Rise up and begin to walk on top of it.

—Harold Loomis, in August Wilson's
Joe Turner's Come and Gone

Those African persons in "Middle Passage" were literally sus-
pended in the "oceanic," if we think of the latter in its Freudian
orientation as an analogy for undifferentiated identity: removed
from the indigenous land and culture, and not-yet "American"
either, these captive persons, without names that their captors
would recognize, were in movement across the Atlantic, but
they were also nowhere at all. Inasmuch as, on any given day,

we might imagine, the captive did not know where s/he was, we could say that they were culturally "unmade," thrown in the midst of a figurative darkness that "exposed" their destinies to an unknown course.

—Hortense Spillers, "Mama's Baby, Papa's Maybe: An American Grammar Book"

In the darkest recesses of the deep sea, altogether impractical colors take hold. Purples, greens, and yellows that exist for no discernible reason, shades and hues that serve no evolutionary purpose one might easily trace given the utter lack of light, the absence of photons that might make such traits beneficial to a given creature's duration. I would like to suggest that the capacious, irreducible blackness found at the bottom of the ocean, as well as the myriad forms of uncanny life we observe there once we dare to look—dragonfish with appendages that end in the shimmer of a bright green bulb, *Vampyroteuthis infernalis* with its twin rows of teeth like razor wire adorning each side—serves as an occasion for thinking about the relationship between blackness as a means of organizing both human and nonhuman life (that is, the color line as the human-animal divide *by another name*) and the social lives of the nonhuman animal entities that dwell within the oceanic realm. For even if we turn away from the very depths of the water and train our gaze on its surface, we will find a history of violent proximity between the people who are called black and the nonhuman animals who roam the waves. Though this proximity does not *begin* with the institution of chattel slavery in the Americas, it is from that nodal point in the ever-expanding archive of African diasporic letters—as well as that foundational

moment in the development of the modern world economy and
ecology—that this particular study takes flight. We will begin in
the hold of the ship and move from there to a consideration of
what the sea and its animal life-worlds make possible for the
black literary imagination—what they potentially, or necessarily,
foreclose.

How does the ever-present specter of the transatlantic slave
trade—what we might think of, following Saidiya Hartman and
others, as the afterlife of slavery—propel us to theorize black ecopoetics not as a matter of *ground* but as an occasion to think at the
intersection of terra firma and open sea, surface and benthos, the
observable ocean and the uncharted blackness of its very bottom?[1]
Given recent critical attention paid to African American nature
writing in anthologies such as Camille Dungy's *Black Nature,* as
well as academic monographs including Ian Finseth's *Shades
of Green: Visions of Nature in the Literature of American Slavery,*
Dianne Glave's *Rooted in the Earth: Reclaiming the African American
Environmental Heritage,* and Paul Outka's *Race and Nature: From
Transcendentalism to the Harlem Renaissance,* among others, I am
interested in how we might think alongside black writers who have
historically taken up oceanic ecology, and their necessarily strained
relationship to it, as a central concern.[2] Specifically, in the body of
this chapter, I will concentrate on the writings of two major
twentieth-century African American poets, Robert Hayden and
Melvin Tolson, toward the end of elaborating a theory of black
ecopoetics gone offshore. I will undertake this project primarily
through investigating the ways that both poets deploy sharks in
their writing about the long historical reach of antiblackness as a
dominant structure of feeling, as well as the ongoing presence of
black persistence and black fugitive possibility.

The first section of the chapter is concerned with Robert Hayden's "Middle Passage" and investigates a set of scenes in which sharks are invoked as a means through which to illuminate the particular, peculiar horrors of everyday life aboard the slave ship. In the universe that Hayden fashions, sharks function as a central component of a broader network of living and nonliving actors—the boat crew, the chains, the slave ship itself—which make up what we might think of as a fundamentally antiblack ecosystem. Sharks represent the ever-present threat of imminent death for the enslaved during their time at sea. Yet and still, the enslaved characters in "Middle Passage" are able to leverage the threat of being killed by sharks—effectively reimagining a site of great peril as a means of escape—in order to rebel against the slavers and ultimately to undermine the terms of their captivity. Thus, by way of examining scholarship concerned with the experiences of enslaved persons forced to live through, and engineer a kind of life in spite of, the gratuitous violence endemic to living aboard the slave ship, I argue that the scenes in which sharks appear in "Middle Passage" provide us with useful instruments for theorizing black resistance on the open sea.

The second section of the chapter is an analysis of Melvin Tolson's poem "The Sea-Turtle and the Shark." I am interested here in examining the central narrative thread of the poem, wherein a sea turtle is consumed by a shark and subsequently burrows through its stomach to freedom. This operates, I argue, as a metonym for the myriad ways that black persons are made to navigate the interlocking systems of domination that give shape and form to white civil society and the US American nation-state in particular. In Tolson's vision, blackness is always on the move, always pushing back in ways seen and unseen against a much broader set of op-

erations that seek to curtail life at every turn. In the end, I argue,
Tolson offers us a robust, *fleshly* image of black liberation through
the sea turtle, one that honors the power of revolutionary violence
and refuses to flatten or romanticize the sheer duration of the black
freedom struggle.

Finally, I will pivot in the coda to this chapter by turning
toward the contemporary poet Xandria Phillips's poem "For a Burial
Free of Sharks." I argue that Phillips's poem presents a vision of
black sociality that works to further complicate the visions we
gather from Hayden and Tolson as it pertains to the potential interplay of black life on the ship and the presence of the sharks in
the water below. In Phillips's hands, the slave ship becomes a space
from which we might launch a critique of *the overrepresentation of
Man* as the only meaningful genre of human life and, what is more,
the dominant configuration of the human body itself as always already independent and autonomous.[3] "For a Burial Free of Sharks"
asks us instead to embrace the swarm or the school (in the dou-
bled sense that an aquatic register demands), over and against an
individualized subject position or self; it asks that we reckon with
the possibility of becoming multiple, that we might better understand how the enslaved survived the hold, what they transformed
it into, and what such transformation means for how we imagine
sociality *as such*. In sum, my goal in analyzing this constellation of
texts is to elucidate a divergent approach to the work of thinking
at the intersections of black studies, animality studies, and ecocriticism, to turn toward the sea that we might unsettle the sort of
historical terracentrism that obscures the social and political
possibilities of a wetter archive, a black hydropoetics that does not
require solid ground in order to make its claims or sustain its
movement but rather relishes the freedom of the open water,

dodges death at every turn, makes hazy the division between person and nonperson so that a more robust, ethical lexicon for black life might rise to the air.

❀

From the opening lines of Robert Hayden's "Middle Passage," it creates a world in which the boundaries between animate and inanimate, human and nonhuman, living and dead, are thrown into crisis. The poem's primary setting is a manned ship at sea, the *Amistad*—or, from another angle, what we might also read as many ships operating under the metonymic reach of a single dreamscape, indistinguishable from one another against the haze of the speaker's memory—which famously bore human chattel as its primary cargo:[4]

> *Jesús, Estrella, Esperanza, Mercy:*
> Sails flashing to the wind like weapons,
> sharks following the moans the fever and the dying;
> horror the corposant and compass rose.
> Middle Passage:
> voyage through death
> to life upon these shores.
> "10 April 1800—
> Blacks rebellious. Crew uneasy. Our linguist says
> their moaning is a prayer for death,
> ours and their own. Some try to starve themselves.
> Lost three this morning leaped with crazy laughter
> to the waiting sharks, sang as they went under."
> *Deep in the festering hold thy father lies*
> *of his bones New England pews are made,*
> *those are altar lights that were his eyes.*[5]

The reader is presented here with an image of the slave ship as not only a site of unrelenting violence but one in which species boundaries are crossed as a *direct by-product* of such brutality. The migratory patterns of the sharks in this passage are transformed in the wake of blood spilled from the decks of the seaborne vessel, their every movement altered by the brutal scenes taking place above the surface of the water. The ineluctable irony of each ship's name lands like a blade: *Jesus, Estrella, Esperanza, Mercy,* all transcendent principles or else celestial beings, gods and stars and holy affect, all of which belie the muck and grime of the hold, the labor carried out under banners that to many people might have signified another, higher world, one altogether incompatible with the degradation that serves as the slave ship's condition of emergence. The first set of sharks in this opening scene are merely one component of a much larger network of ultraviolent actors that Hayden draws our attention to from the outset. Even the sails are instruments of war, "flashing . . . like weapons" as sharks dart through the current below. The compass rose is fear itself. Everywhere, in Hayden's landscape, terror reigns, and human beings are not the only ones that serve as its enacting agents.

The entire ship, as well as the broader environment surrounding it, comes alive and works in tandem to create what we might envision, to invoke Stephanie Smallwood's work, as a kind of living death for every enslaved person onboard.[6] In this sense, the very phrase "Middle Passage," it seems, connotes both a literal movement along the routes of the transatlantic slave trade over the course of several centuries and an intermediary category betwixt living and dying that is not a space of limbo so much as the fusion of both planes into something like a deathly persistence—a mode of existing outside the boundaries and protections of the genre of

Man and thus in closer, generative proximity to nonhuman life forms. It is during this process, while being forced to move through the countless, day-to-day violences endemic to life aboard the ship, that the enslaved Africans who serve as Hayden's primary points of concern first learn what it will mean to live as black nonpersons, Negroes, the objects against which the utopian vision of a life worth living on the very shores he describes will come to be oppositionally defined.

Rather than accepting such a fate with quiet resignation, the enslaved characters in "Middle Passage" rebel from the very first, striking back against their captors in order to take the vessel as their own. Sharks are part and parcel of this collective resistance; the insurgents that Hayden describes leap overboard once it is clear that there is no rebellion that can be waged and won on the decks of the ship. Marcus Rediker writes about this historical practice— that is, of enslaved insurgents deploying suicide as a means of resisting the conditions of their bondage—in his seminal study *Outlaws of the Atlantic: Sailors, Pirates, and Motley Crews in the Age of Sail:*

> Some jumped in the hope of escape while docked in an African port, while others chose drowning over starvation as a means to terminate the life of the body meant to slave away on New World Plantations. This kind of resistance was widely practiced and just as widely feared by the organizers of the trade. Merchants warned captains about it in their instructions, formal and informal. Captains in turn made sure their ships had nettings all around. They also had the male captives chained to a ring bolt whenever they were on the main deck, and at the same time made sure that vigilant watches were always kept. . . . One of the most illuminating

aspects of these suicidal escapes was the joy expressed by people once they had gotten into the water. Seaman Isaac Wilson recalled a captive who jumped into the sea and "went down as if exalting that he got away."[7]

Not unlike Hayden's vision of the affective economies and exchanges that characterized the Middle Passage for the enslaved, what Rediker describes here is a social world in which any and all approaches to opposition are at play, means that also include leveraging the presence of nonhuman animal actors toward the end of *stealing oneself away*, refusing to become the property of another even if that choice ends in death. Sharks, which are described in the preceding section of "Middle Passage" as simultaneously *waiting* and *following*, thus function as a kind of specter, both an ever-looming threat to the flourishing of black life and a release valve, a guaranteed exit. This is especially important given all of the precautions taken by slavers—the aforementioned netting around ships, for example—to ensure that the black human beings onboard lived long enough to be appraised and sold. Of critical import here also is the role of West African cosmologies and spiritual practice as it pertains to the enslaved and their vision of what it might mean to steal away; many saw biological death not as an absolute conclusion but rather as a means of returning to one's native land.[8]

Stealing oneself away was a refusal of objectification, an unmooring of the relentless, necromantic machinations of a global order that demanded human beings be transformed into saleable commodities. Over and against the lethal pressures of global white supremacy, the men and women whom Hayden describes herein dared to imagine a second home beyond the sea, life and death by other names. The afterlife of such thinking can be found, it bears mentioning, within the realm of twentieth- and twenty-first-century black expressive cultures. The Detroit-based electronic band Drexciya, for instance, constructed an entire mythology around just such a vision of black social life beneath the sea.[9] In the sleeve notes of the band's 1997 album, *The Quest*, the electronic music duo—composed of James Stinson and Gerald Donald—first began to fashion an origin story wherein the band's name is said also to be that of an entire underwater country, one founded by the children of enslaved women thrown overboard, women whose children developed the ability to breathe water in utero, survived, and went on to found something akin to a black Atlantis, an underwater utopia far more advanced in its technology, and its ethics, than any civilization on land. This notion of an underwater refuge for black people is also reflected in the works of other artists such as Sun Ra, the experimental film collective the Otolith Group, and the visual artist Ellen Gallagher.[10] In all of these works, the haunting presence of the Middle Passage is recalibrated toward the end of imagining an elsewhere, however remote or deeply submerged, where black life can flourish. Conceptualizing a black Atlantis is labor that unsettles the terracentrism of our political imaginations, threatens the seeming interminability of the land-borne nation-state, and demands a more dynamic approach to organizing life on Earth. Gratuitous violence is alchemized in the light of the black fantastic, allowing for new practices of being together to emerge.[11] When we immerse ourselves within this archive, we find both otherworldly despair and fugitive possibility—uncharted, undercommon marronage made possible by the opacity of the oceanic realm.[12]

In this vein, the outpouring of exuberant affect that both Hayden and Rediker describe in the moments when enslaved persons begin to sink below the surface of the sea also demands our attention. How do we make sense of such unfettered emotion on this occasion? The captive gives his very suffering over to the tide, and all he can do is exalt, the slaver's power torn asunder at last by laughter. This refusal to be transmogrified into property without will or imagination, especially as reflected in the act of giving one's flesh to the water, is a theme of critical import throughout "Middle Passage" and is most forcefully articulated toward the end of the poem's first section, where sharks yet again make an appearance, though in a fashion that veers somewhat from their role earlier on:

> Misfortune
> follows in our wake like sharks (our grinning
> tutelary gods). Which one of us
> has killed an albatross? A plague among
> our blacks—Ophthalmia: blindness—& we
> have jettisoned the blind to no avail.
> It spreads, the terrifying sickness spreads.
> Its claws have scratched sight from the Capt.'s eyes
> & there is blindness in the fo'c'sle
> & we must sail 3 weeks before we come to port.
> *What port awaits us, Davy Jones'*
> *or home? I've heard of slavers drifting, drifting,*
> *playthings of wind and storm and chance, their crews*
> *gone blind, the jungle hatred*
> *crawling up on deck.*[13]

Here, the aforementioned sharks transition from being invoked as physical threats to human life to serving as metaphors for the broader set of troubles that pursue the ship and its crew. And though the primary focus of this section is a wave of ophthalmia that overtakes the boat's inhabitants, we might also read the invocation of the sharks here as a reversal in polarity, that is, the sharks as a source of fear and imminent danger for the white crewmen *as opposed to the enslaved*. This shift represents a critical turn in the narrative trajectory of "Middle Passage." The speaker's referring to the sharks as *grinning gods*, for example, works to invert the myth of whiteness as "the ownership of the world forever and ever," whiteness as immortality.[14] No one here evades the grave. Following this section, the sharks disappear, and there is no guardian remaining to protect the white crewmen. The "jungle hatred" described by the speaker reads almost as a plague of some higher origin, the embodiment of the rage of the enslaved, and a harbinger of the destruction to come in the poem's second section. In these final two movements, the ship is taken over in an act of outright insurrection, the captain and crew slain by the insurgents formerly resigned to life in the hold.

This portion of the text is meant to directly mirror the most well-known historical accounts of the insurgency aboard the *Amistad* and, in doing so, grounds us in a historical archive of slave rebellion made legible by the invocation of the names of the rebels themselves, most notably Cinquez, whom Hayden describes in the poem's last lines as the "deathless primaveral image" of human freedom's "timeless will," a "life that transfigures many lives."[15] In the poem's concluding scene, the grinning shark gods—as well as the crew of slavers we might think of as made in their very image, or else acolytes of their storied rage, voracious hunger—are done away with in the name of an alternate eschatology, one in which the spirit of a certain black radicalism prevails over the unchecked cruelty of the slave system, its endless tentacles that extend even into the social lives of animals. As Hayden demonstrates, a rig-

orous accounting of chattel slavery and its afterlives demands that
we engage nonhuman life-worlds, that we recognize the work of
Afro-diasporic ecopoetics, and black study more broadly, as *species thinking*, as ecological thought at the end of the world.[16]

❁

> I learned that the shark and the slave trade had gone to-
> gether from the beginning. Indeed, one of the prevailing
> theories about the origin of the term "shark" in English can
> be traced back to the first English slaving voyages to West
> Africa, led by Captain John Hawkins during the 1560s.
> When someone captured, killed, and brought to London
> one of the huge creatures in 1569, the people of the city stood
> amazed but knew not what to call the "marueilous straunge
> Fishe." According to sixteenth-century ballads and broad-
> sides, "sertayne men of Captayne Haukinses doth call it a
> sharke." "Shark" thus seems to have entered the English lan-
> guage through the talk of slave-trade sailors, who may have
> picked up and adapted the word "xoc," pronounced "choke,"
> from the Maya in the Caribbean. "Shark" would soon take
> its place in the lexicon of class description, a cant term sig-
> nifying a worthless fellow who made a living by his wits,
> sponging, swindling, cheating, and scamming.
>
> —Marcus Rediker, "History from Below the Water Line:
> Sharks and the Atlantic Slave Trade"

The twentieth-century poet and critic Melvin Tolson's "The Sea-
Turtle and the Shark" is an altogether brief yet striking meditation
on the shape and tenor of black social life in modernity, a harrowing
account of how it feels to navigate a world in which one is forced
to live daily under the threat of violence that is not aberrational
but *algorithmic*, built right into the code of the contemporary
social order.[17] Tolson's poem intervenes as an alternative cartog-
raphy of the present, a set of instructions as to how one might

survive when one is, to use Stokely Carmichael's turn of phrase, born in jail.[18] From the outset of the poem, readers find themselves forced to look outward from the confines of an enclosure:

> Strange but true is the story
> of the sea-turtle and the shark—
> the instinctive drive of the weak to survive
> in the oceanic dark.
> Driven,
> riven
> by hunger
> from abyss to shoal,
> sometimes the shark swallows
> the sea-turtle whole.[19]

We are introduced to the sea turtle as a character that serves as the embodiment of "the weak," a broader network of actors whose survival is marked throughout as unceasing labor, an ongoing refusal of the normative order of things. Indeed, readers are forewarned that what they are about to read is a "strange but true" story. This strangeness demands our attention, that is, the particular set of inversions deployed by Tolson in order to use the sea turtle as a metonym for black experience. The inside of the shark's body is a darkness within darkness, a blackness born of the deep in which normative hierarchies are destabilized.

Tolson's imagery in this portion of the poem can also be read as a gesture toward the biblical narrative of Jonah and the giant fish. Within the context of that particular tale—which merits an abridged retelling if only for the sake of clarifying the extent of Tolson's rather subtle riff—Jonah's extended interment in the fish's body is the product of his refusal to follow a direct command from the mouth of God: a call to preach the need for repentance to the denizens of the city of Nineveh. Jonah eventually takes flight and boards a ship full of other fugitives in hopes of evading divine commission. His plan—doomed perhaps from the very start, rooted as it was in evading the will of the sovereign in plain sight—fails spectacularly. An especially vicious squall strikes while he and his fellow crewmen are at sea, a catastrophe that he reads as a sign that he must repent and accept punishment for his attempt at rebellion. He asks that his body be cast overboard, a last-ditch plan to evade the wrath of the divine. This time, Jonah's gambit is a successful one, though not in the way he expects; the storm quiets, and everyone onboard the ship lives. But rather than drowning, and in the process giving over his life in an act of penance, Jonah is swallowed by a giant fish, lives in its stomach for several days, and is eventually spit up on land, finally prepared to undertake the evangelical labor to which he had been called days earlier.

Tolson reworks this tale toward radical ends. The rest of the poem reads as follows:

> The sly reptilian marine
> withdraws,
> into the shell
> of his undersea craft,
> his leathery head and the rapacious claws
> that can rip
> a rhinoceros' hide
> or strip
> a crocodile to fare-thee well;
> now,
> *inside* the shark,

the sea-turtle begins the churning seesaws
of his descent into pelagic hell;
then . . . *then,*
with ravenous jaws
that can cut sheet steel scrap,
the sea-turtle gnaws
. . . and gnaws . . . and gnaws
his way in a way that appalls—
his way to freedom,
beyond the vomiting dark beyond the stomach walls
of the shark.[20]

The story of Jonah and the giant fish thus becomes an allegory put
to revolutionary use, a black radical operation with a nonhuman
actor at its center. Herein, the forms of life trapped in the black-
ening depths of the leviathan's belly are not rescued by the workings of a watchful sovereign. They suffer and are not saved. Instead,
the sea turtle uses all that it has at its disposal, its very flesh, to
tear a pathway through the body of the shark, which, for Tolson,
stands in for the interlocking systems of domination that serve as
civil society's architecture. The sea turtle does not, cannot, wait to
be rescued. It takes its freedom back through a gradual cutting
away at the material foundations of its cage. Held firmly within
the belly of the shark and nonetheless alive, Tolson's sea turtle provides us with a theory of black fugitivity in the flesh of the animal, its persistent burrowing a model for how we might enact our
freedom dreams though we might be hunted, hamstrung, surrounded on all sides. Notice too how Tolson invokes an entire
bestiary full of larger creatures in order to emphasize the sheer
power of the sea turtle's bite, its largely unheralded *capacity for de-*

struction. Crocodiles and rhinoceroses alike are cited as no real match for the sea turtle's hidden power; both are invoked as a means of making a certain argument against appearance, against the utility of possessing brute strength alone.

Rather, it is precisely the size and otherwise advantageous attributes of the crocodile, the rhinoceros, and the shark that bars them from the sort of life-worlds available to the sea turtle, which is underestimated, demeaned, seen as little more than raw matter fit for consumption. From this position at the very bottom of the hierarchy, the sea turtle attacks, gains its freedom, and also, readers are led to believe, mortally wounds that which depends on its destruction for sustenance. The sea turtle's work, the speaker tells us, is *appalling.* It is not quick or pristine. It reminds us, per Fred Moten and Saidiya Hartman's recent commentary in "The Black Outdoors," that fugitive practice is inherently processual, that escape is not an achievement but an *activity.*[21] The rigorous push toward liberation as it is framed by "The Sea-Turtle and the Shark" is an altogether bloody affair and takes place in a space of what many would call nothingness. These are the conditions from which abolitionist instruments emerge. This is how, and where, one develops the meditative tenacity needed to slice the machine clean through. Envisioning resistance, for Tolson, begins with those who have been all but completely consumed by the present order, the ones detained, held in suspension, never allowed to breathe. Rather than begin with the birds of the air or even the various forms of animal being and becoming that can be found beneath the surface of the earth, Tolson elects to turn toward the sea that he might imagine black flight anew. He transports the hold from the surface of the ocean to its very underbelly. And there, in the absence of light or human life, he sketches a world wherein the shark, the very embodiment of an antiblack social order—and thus, it follows, precisely the sort of exploitative, exorbitantly violent figure that Rediker's etymology gestures toward—is decimated from within, laid to waste by the least of these, the drowned and yet undead.

❁

(I suffer, I am that man anonymous in the waves)
—Rickey Laurentiis, "Mood for Love"

Xandria Phillips's "For a Burial Free of Sharks" attends as its central objects of inquiry to people who, to use Mariame Kaba's phrase, *had no selves to defend,* those whose very living served as a critique of selfhood.[22] The poem's first lines provide a critical language for the experience of utter fungibility, which is also always to say, black life within the confines of the hold:

> in the hull we worked we wormed at earth's lack in we lives and
> in those deaths / and I say we / not collective not tongued the same
> and not kin and not in love / but in all of we pressed up against
> we heat and doings similar and reduced to sameness / saw the first
> of we plunging for home / . . . / we risked death to put dead in the
> ground[23]

The figures that Phillips invokes have no access to any legible form of individualized personhood. What takes its place, at least within the world of the poem, is an echoing *we,* a refrain that doubles as a critique of Man, an unmooring of any singular, autonomous speaker. Over and against a dominant, Lockean vision of personhood in which a given body—as Monique Allewaert reminds us—is imagined as a "single, self-identical and particular consciousness that persists despite the diverse materials, things, temporalities, and places that press upon it and pass through it," the speaker of "For a Burial Free of Sharks" enacts a vision of personhood that is *inherently* multiple.[24] That is, it is a vision of human becoming akin to what Frantz Fanon describes in "The Fact of Blackness" as *inner kinship*, the sense that blacks are not unitary beings but multitudinous, always already representing not only themselves as individual actors but a larger, diasporic conglomerate, as well as one's deceased ancestors, during any given moment of racialized encounter.[25]

One hears echoes of Fanon in the speaker's invocation of a people that are "not kin" but "reduced to sameness." The lived experience of this *reduction*—the social practices and protocols, the black operations that emerge from such brutality—is a central focus of the poem. This emphasis is expressed most poignantly perhaps in the speaker's claim that those who were forced to live in the hold were willing to sacrifice their very lives in order to honor the dead. On the funereal practices of the enslaved, Vincent Brown writes,

> The death rite thus enabled them to express and enact their social values, to articulate their visions of what it was that bound them together, made individuals among them unique, and separated this group of people from others. The scene . . . typifies the way that people who have been pronounced socially dead, that is, utterly alienated and with no social ties recognized as legitimate or binding, have often made a social world out of death itself. The funeral was an act of accounting, of reckoning, and therefore one among the multitude of acts that made up the political history of Atlantic slavery. This was politics conceived not as a conventional battle between partisans, but as a struggle to define a social being that connected the past and present.[26]

Following Brown, then, we can imagine the space of the hold in "For a Burial Free of Sharks" as one in which the enslaved came to bend and blur the division that demarcates life and death as such. The world of the poem offers a space of indeterminacy in which there is no need for earth in order to bury the deceased, no ground to dig up or stand on, ontological or otherwise. One might argue in fact, as Jonathan Howard does, that "slaves in the hold may be understood to have constituted the ground upon which whiteness could originally stand and purport to be."[27] For both Brown and Howard, then, there is a kind of life beyond life, a form of being without borders, that finds expression in the hold. From within the irreparable break engendered by the instantiation of the transatlantic slave trade, the ever-expanding caesura that has many names but no sufficient description, there emerges a critique of Western civilization that extends far beyond the slave ship. In the absence of ground, the enslaved imagine and enact a modality that operates under radically divergent principles: a grammar of the flesh.

The question of groundlessness, or rather, another sort of ground altogether, is central and reappears explicitly in the poem's final movement:

> but tides did rise and sharks plowed what we hands put over we / found we bodies to devour / failure to send we home was not without punishment / one of we / not I was tethered / ankle to hull / and we saw this one we disappear by limb until there was only a pair of feet trailing the ship / I still haven't a want for death / and I know my burial impends / we all been too physical / our flesh is the closest ground in sight / putting the mind on a high shelf is a burial without sharks / I double where my joints can and bury self in self[28]

At long last, in these closing lines, the eponymous sharks swerve into the frame. In the first instance, they seem to operate in a vein not unlike those of Hayden's "Middle Passage," that is, as a persistent, existential threat to the lives of the captives. The second time they appear, however, the sharks are more or less immaterial, more an abstract illustration of the continuous threat to black life that modernity represents than any discrete danger. The speaker claims that something like a *natural death*—one without the spectacular violence that so often attends black mortality—is only possible through placing the mind "on a high shelf," one far higher, we might imagine, than even the topmost corners of the hold, higher than the walls of any cage in the world. Thus, the dream of a burial free of sharks is not just the dream of black life lived beyond the reach of the bull's-eye. Rather, it is enacted in the everyday social practices, and *mentation*, of those who know that the sharks are everywhere and always in relentless pursuit, those who nonetheless look to the blackness of the deep and dare to proclaim that they are likewise unfathomable, untamable, endless.

NOTES

Introduction

Epigraph: Richard Wright, "The Literature of the Negro in the United States," in *Black Power: Three Books from Exile: Black Power; The Color Curtain; and White Man, Listen!* (New York: HarperCollins, 2010), 1371.

1. Frederick Douglass, *Narrative of the Life of Frederick Douglass, an American Slave* (Boston: Bedford/St. Martin's, 2003), 1.
2. Frederick Douglass, "Agriculture and Black Progress," in *The Frederick Douglass Papers, Series One: Speeches, Debates, and Interviews,* ed. John W. Blassingame and John R. McKivigan (New Haven, CT: Yale University Press, 1979), 388.
3. John Berger, *Why Look at Animals?* (London: Penguin, 2009).
4. Lucille Clifton, *Good News about the Earth: New Poems* (New York: Random House, 1972), 2.
5. See Countee Cullen, *The Lost Zoo,* illus. Joseph Low (Chicago: Follett, 1969).
6. See Henry Bibb, *The Life and Adventures of Henry Bibb: An American Slave, Written by Himself* (Urbana, IL: Project Gutenberg), 46.
7. W. E. B. Du Bois, *The Souls of Black Folk Essays and Sketches* (Charlottesville: University of Virginia Library, 1996), 64.
8. Audre Lorde, "A Litany for Survival," in *Bomb* 56 (1996).

9. Toni Morrison, *Beloved* (New York: Knopf, 1987), 166.

10. Michel Serres, *The Natural Contract* (Ann Arbor: University of Michigan Press, 1985), 38.

11. For more on black ecology, see Nathan Hare, "Black Ecology," *The Black Scholar* 1, no. 6 (1970): 2–8.

12. See Georg Wilhelm Friedrich Hegel, *Philosophy of Right,* trans. T. M. Knox (Oxford: Oxford University Press, 1967), 303.

13. Henry Campbell Black, *Black's Law Dictionary* (St. Paul, MN: West, 1968), 1300.

14. See Katherine McKittrick, ed., *Sylvia Wynter: On Being Human as Praxis* (Durham, NC: Duke University Press, 2015).

15. See Christina Sharpe, *In the Wake: On Blackness and Being* (Durham, NC: Duke University Press, 2016), 102.

16. See Abdul R. JanMohamed, *The Death-Bound-Subject: Richard Wright's Archaeology of Death* (Durham NC: Duke University Press, 2005), 85.

17. See Afaa M. Weaver, "American Income," in *The Plum Flower Dance: Poems 1985 to 2005* (Pittsburgh: University of Pittsburgh Press, 2007), 43.

18. For more on what I am thinking of here as "vitalized forms of death," see Jared Sexton, "The Social Life of Social Death: On Afro-Pessimism and Black Optimism," *InTensions* 5 (2011): 1–47.

1. Rat

Epigraphs: Clapperton Chakanetsa Mavhunga, "Vermin Beings: On Pestiferous Animals and Human Game," *Social Text* 29, no. 1 (106) (2011): 153; Major Jackson, "Pest," *Callaloo* 22, no. 4 (1999): 986; Nathan Fenno, "Clippers Owner Is No Stranger to Race-Related Lawsuits," *Los Angeles Times,* April 26, 2014.

1. See Abdul R. JanMohamed, *The Death-Bound-Subject: Richard Wright's Archaeology of Death* (Durham, NC: Duke University Press, 2005), 85.

2. Rory Putman, *Mammals as Pests* (London: Chapman and Hall, 1989), 1.

3. Spencer D. C. Keralis, "Feeling Animal: Pet-Making and Mastery in the *Slave's Friend*," *American Periodicals: A Journal of History, Criticism, and Bibliography* 22, no. 2 (2012): 124.

4. Tara Betts, "For Those Who Need a True Story," in *Black Nature: Four Centuries of African American Nature Poetry,* ed. Camille T. Dungy (Athens: University of Georgia Press, 2009), 124.

5. See Tim Seibles, "Ambition II: Mosquito in the Mist," in *Buffalo Head Solos: Poems* (Cleveland: Cleveland State University Poetry Center, 2004), 97.

6. Betts, "For Those Who Need a True Story," 125.

7. Sylvia Hood Washington, *Packing Them In: An Archaeology of Environmental Racism in Chicago, 1865–1954* (Lanham, MD: Lexington Books, 2005), 26.

8. Richard Wright, *Native Son* (New York: Harper and Bros., 1940), 10.

9. Michael Lundblad, *The Birth of a Jungle: Animality in Progressive-Era U.S. Literature and Culture* (Oxford: Oxford University Press, 2013), 122.

10. Richard Wright, *12 Million Black Voices* (New York: Thunder's Mouth, 1941), 111.

11. Ibid.

12. Clare Eby, "Slouching toward Beastliness: Richard Wright's Anatomy of Thomas Dixon," *African American Review* 35, no. 3 (2001): 439.

13. Wright, *Native Son*, 448.

14. Here I am thinking through and alongside Fred Moten's talk on April 22, 2013, at Tramway in Glasgow: "Well. You just caught me giving them something I shouldn't be giving them. We don't want to give them anything we might want later. There's that Howlin' Wolf song, where he says, he says maybe we might want to hold on to evil. Yeah, we might need that. So maybe let's not give them anything. Let's not give them any adjectives. Let's just say there's something wrong with them. Let's just call them bosses and leave it at that."

15. James Smethurst, "Invented by Horror: The Gothic and African American Literary Ideology in *Native Son*," *African American Review* 35, no. 1 (2001): 36.

16. For are not those morning conversations through which we are first introduced to Vera, Bigger's mother, and the rest of the family evidence of an everyday persistence that must be recognized and reckoned with? Is this not something other than emptiness or vain clawing for survival? Such phonic materiality produces something other than what Smethurst and others want to claim as empty space.

17. Smethurst, "Invented by Horror," 36.

18. Ibid.

19. Wright, *Native Son*, 13.

20. Ibid., 9.

21. Ibid.

22. Sam Bluefarb, *The Escape Motif in the American Novel: Mark Twain to Richard Wright* (Columbus: Ohio State University Press, 1972), 136–137.

23. Ibid., 136.

24. Ibid.

25. For more on the centrality of flight to Bigger's characterization in *Native Son*, see Mikko Tukhanen, "Avian Alienation: Writing and Flying in Wright and Lacan," in *The American Optic: Psychoanalysis, Critical Race Theory, and Richard Wright* (Albany: State University of New York Press, 2009), 133–168.

26. Jonathan Burt, *Rat* (London: Reaktion Books, 2006), 12–13.

27. See Giorgio Agamben, *Homo Sacer* (Stanford, CA: Stanford University Press, 1998).

28. Wright, *Native Son*, 264–265.

29. Burt, *Rat*, 7.

30. Wright, *Native Son*, 265.

31. Abdul R. JanMohamed, *The Death-Bound-Subject: Richard Wright's Archaeology of Death* (Durham NC: Duke University Press, 2005), 85.

32. I borrow the term "third space" from Homi K. Bhabha. For more on third space, see Bhabha, *The Location of Culture* (London: Routledge, 1994).

33. JanMohamed, *Death-Bound-Subject*, 85.

34. Charles W. Mills, *The Racial Contract* (Ithaca, NY: Cornell University Press, 1997), 97.

35. I borrow the term "good life" from Lauren Berlant. See Lauren Berlant, *Cruel Optimism* (Durham, NC: Duke University Press, 2011).

36. Leza Lowitz, review of *Haiku: This Other World*, by Richard Wright, *Manoa* 13, no. 2 (2001): 204.

37. Julia Wright, introduction to *Haiku: This Other World*, by Richard Wright (New York: Arcade, 1998), 8.

38. For readers interested in a text in which Wright's haiku appear as part of a much larger cycle dedicated to the relationship between African American poets and pest animals, see Dungy, *Black Nature*.

39. Constance Webb, *Richard Wright* (New York: G. P. Putnam's Sons, 1968), 387, 393–394.

40. Ibid., 6.

41. Ibid., 19.

42. Ibid., 29.

43. Floyd Ogburn, "Richard Wright's Unpublished Haiku: A World Elsewhere," *Melus* 23, no. 3 (1998): 58.

44. Richard Iadonisi, "'I Am Nobody': The Haiku of Richard Wright," *Melus* 30, no. 3 (2005): 191.

45. Ibid.

46. See Robert Tener, "The Where, the When, the What: A Study of Richard Wright's Haiku," in *Critical Essays on Richard Wright,* ed. Yoshinobu Hakutani (Boston: G. K. Hall, 1982), 273–298.

47. Wright, *Haiku,* 113.

2. Cock

Epigraphs: Afaa Michael Weaver, "American Income," *Poetry* 189, no. 6 (2007): 465; Daniel Patrick Moynihan, *The Negro Family: The Case for National Action,* in *The Moynihan Report and the Politics of Controversy,* by Lee Rainwater and William L. Yancey (Cambridge, MA: MIT Press, 1967), 16; Langston Hughes, "Dreams," in *The Collected Poems of Langston Hughes* (New York: Vintage, 2020), 32.

1. For more on the relationship between black masculinity and (social / civic) death, see both Thelma Golden, *Black Male: Representations of Masculinity in Contemporary American Art* (New York: Whitney Museum of American Art, 1994); and Orlando Patterson, *Slavery and Social Death: A Comparative Study* (Cambridge, MA: Harvard University Press, 1982).

2. See Rosemarie Garland Thomson, *Extraordinary Bodies: Figuring Physical Disability in American Culture and Literature* (New York: Columbia University Press, 1997), for a singular example of this sort of rigorous interdisciplinary work on Morrison.

3. See Afaa M. Weaver, "American Income," in *The Plum Flower Dance: Poems 1985 to 2005* (Pittsburgh: University of Pittsburgh Press, 2007), 43.

4. Nahum D. Chandler, "Of Exorbitance: The Problem of the Negro as a Problem for Thought," *Criticism* 50, no. 3 (2009): 345–410.

5. Toni Morrison, *Song of Solomon* (New York: Plume, 1987), 3.

6. Ibid.

7. Ibid., 9.

8. Ibid., 8.

9. Ibid., 9.

10. A relatively small sampling of Morrison's novels bears this out: Chicken Little, Son, Yardman, Baby Suggs, Eva Peace, Paul D, Denver, and Pecola Breedlove are just a few of the names that illustrate this point.

11. Morrison, *Song of Solomon*, 330.

12. Ibid., 9.

13. Ibid., 9.

14. Jacques Lacan, "The Mirror Stage as Formative of the *I* Function as Revealed in Psychoanalytic Experience," in *Écrits: The First Complete Edition in English*, trans. Bruce Fink (New York: Norton, 2006), 76.

15. For more on grievable life, see Judith Butler, *Frames of War: When Is Life Grievable?* (London: Verso, 2009).

16. Morrison, *Song of Solomon*, 62–63.

17. Ibid., 17.

18. Ibid., 15.

19. Lena: "Our girlhood was spent like a found nickel on you. When you slept, we were quiet; when you were hungry, we cooked; when you wanted to play, we entertained you; and when you got grown enough to know the difference between a woman and a two-toned Ford, everything in this house stopped for you. You have yet to wash your own underwear, spread a bed, wipe the ring from your tub, or move a fleck of your dirt from one place to another. And to this day, you have never asked one of us if we were tired, or sad, or wanted a cup of coffee. You've never picked up anything heavier than your own feet, or solved a problem harder than fourth-grade arithmetic. Where do you get the *right* to decide our lives? . . . I'll tell you where. From that hog's gut that hangs down between your legs. Well, let me tell you something, baby brother: you will need more than that. I don't know where you will get it or who will give it to you, but mark my words, you will need more than that." Ibid., 215.

20. New York Public Library, "Toni Morrison | Junot Díaz," December 13, 2013, www.nypl.org/audiovideo/toni-morrison-junot-d%C3%ADaz.

21. Melissa Gregg and Gregory J. Seigworth, "An Inventory of Shimmers," in *The Affect Theory Reader*, ed. Gregg and Seigworth (Durham, NC: Duke University Press, 2010), 2.

22. This, of course, is a riff on none other than that incomparable theorist of affect and relation Teddy Pendergrass.

23. Morrison, *Song of Solomon*, 26.

24. Ibid., 37.

25. Ibid., 39.

26. Regarding luck, I am thinking of Pilate's unforgettable characterization of her eldest daughter: "Reba wins things. She ain't never lost nothing."

27. Morrison, *Song of Solomon*, 179.

28. Ibid., 179–180.

29. Frantz Fanon, *Black Skin, White Masks* (New York: Grove, 2008), 95.

30. The "wages of whiteness" is a term I am borrowing from the title of David Roediger's book of the same name.

31. It is telling that our first encounter with the figure of the peacock in the novel is not during the exchange between the white peacock and Milkman and Guitar but during a flashback to the moment that Macon, having just killed a man in self-defense, discovers a bag of gold deep within the cave where he and Pilate have been sleeping after their father is murdered: "'Gold,' he whispered, and immediately, like a burglar out on his first job, stood up to pee. Life, safety, and luxury fanned out before him like the tail-spread of a peacock, and as he stood there trying to distinguish each delicious color, he saw the dusty boots of his father standing just on the other side of the shallow pit." Morrison, *Song of Solomon*, 170.

32. "Talk with Toni Morrison: Mel Watkins / 1977," in *Conversations with Toni Morrison*, ed. Danille Kathleen Guthrie (Jackson: University Press of Mississippi, 1994), 45–46.

33. Ibid., 46.

34. Alexander Weheliye, *Habeas Viscus: Racializing Assemblages, Biopolitics, and Black Feminist Theories of the Human* (Durham, NC: Duke University Press, 2014), 4.

35. Daniel Patrick Moynihan, *The Negro Family: The Case for National Action*, in *The Moynihan Report and the Politics of Controversy*, by Lee Rainwater and William L. Yancey (Cambridge, MA: MIT Press, 1967), 29.

36. Ibid., 10.

37. Ibid., 34.

38. Ibid., 16.

39. Lewis R. Gordon, *Bad Faith and Anti-black Racism* (Atlantic Highlands, NJ: Humanities Press, 1995), 124.

40. Regarding the black absentee father, see Jo Jones and William D. Mosher, "Fathers' Involvement with Their Children: United States, 2006–2010," *National Health Statistics Reports* 71 (2013): 1–21.

41. David Marriott, *On Black Men* (Edinburgh: Edinburgh University Press, 2000), 98.

42. James Baldwin and Audre Lorde, "Revolutionary Hope: A Conversation between James Baldwin and Audre Lorde," *Essence*, January 1, 1984.

43. For more on blackness as an incommunicable position, see Frank B. Wilderson III, *Red, White, and Black: Cinema and the Structure of U.S. Antagonisms* (Durham, NC: Duke University Press, 2010).

44. Morrison, *Song of Solomon*, 322–323.
45. Ibid., 222.
46. A number of these forms of male kinship, it should be noted, are marked by the presence of birds, not only the aforementioned peacock but also the moment when "a black rooster strutted by, its blood-red comb draped forward like a wicked brow," right before Milkman gets into a fistfight with a group of men from the area. Ibid., 265.
47. Indeed, this is also the moment when the white peacock appears for the final time. The creature is described by the narrator as soaring away, ultimately alighting on the hood of the blue Buick elsewhere.
48. The following exchange between Milkman and Guitar reflects this broader trend throughout the book: "'Yeah, but except for skin color, I can't tell the difference between what the white women want from us and what the colored women want. You say they all want our life, our living life. So if a colored woman is raped and killed, why do the Days rape and kill a white woman? Why worry about the colored woman at all?' Guitar cocked his head and looked sideways at Milkman. His nostrils flared a little. 'Because she's *mine*.'" Ibid., 223.
49. Ibid., 337.
50. See Langston Hughes, "The Negro Artist and the Racial Mountain," *Langston Hughes Review* 4, no. 1 (1985): 1–4.

3. Mule

Epigraphs: Patricia Hill Collins, *Black Feminist Thought: Knowledge, Consciousness, and the Politics of Empowerment* (New York: Routledge, 2002), 48; Alexander G. Weheliye, *Habeas Viscus: Racializing Assemblages, Biopolitics, and Black Feminist Theories of the Human* (Durham, NC: Duke University Press, 2014), 8; Hortense Spillers, "Mama's Baby, Papa's Maybe: An American Grammar Book," *Diacritics* 17, no. 2 (1987): 65.

1. For more on Linda Brent's use of the epistolary form as a mode of fugitive resistance, see Linda Brent, *Incidents in the Life of a Slave Girl* (Jersey City, NJ: Start, 2013).
2. Here, I am riffing on Audre Lorde's poem "Litany for Survival." For the text in its entirety, see Audre Lorde, "From *A Litany for Survival*," *Bomb* 56 (1996): 34–37.
3. Zora Neale Hurston, *Their Eyes Were Watching God: A Novel* (New York: Perennial Library, 1990), 49.
4. Ibid., 57.

5. Karl Marx, *Capital, Volume 1: A Critique of Political Economy* (Digireads .com, 2004), 303.

6. For "freedom drive," see Fred Moten, *In the Break: The Aesthetics of the Black Radical Tradition* (Minneapolis: University of Minnesota Press, 2003), 7.

7. Hortense J. Spillers, "Mama's Baby, Papa's Maybe: An American Grammar Book," *Diacritics* 17, no. 2 (1987): 64.

8. Ibid., 67.

9. Elizabeth Grosz, "Merleau-Ponty and Irigaray in the Flesh," *Thesis Eleven* 36, no. 1 (1993): 54.

10. Hurston, *Their Eyes Were Watching God: A Novel*, 43.

11. For more on the intersections of gender and ecology in *Their Eyes Were Watching God*, see Paul Outka, *Race and Nature from Transcendentalism to the Harlem Renaissance* (New York: Palgrave Macmillan, 2013).

12. Spillers, "Mama's Baby," 80.

13. Hurston, *Their Eyes Were Watching God*, 68.

14. For historical discourses, see Thomas Jefferson, *Notes on the State of Virginia* (New York: Penguin, 1999). For contemporary discourses, see Orlando Patterson, *Rituals of Blood: Consequences of Slavery in Two American Centuries* (New York: Basic Civitas Books, 1998).

15. Hurston, *Their Eyes Were Watching God*, 93.

16. Ibid., 95.

17. For more on storying as an African American expressive practice, see Kevin Young, *The Grey Album: On the Blackness of Blackness* (New York: Macmillan, 2012).

18. Ibid., 96.

19. Ibid., 32.

20. See Richard Wright, "Between Laughter and Tears," *New Masses* 25 (October 1937): 22–24.

21. For more on the particular distinction between the social and the political that I am calling on here, see Stefano Harney and Fred Moten, *The Undercommons: Fugitive Planning & Black Study* (New York: Minor Compositions, 2013).

22. See Martin Heidegger, *Poetry, Language, Thought* (New York: Harper and Row, 1975), 176.

23. Zora Neale Hurston, *Dust Tracks on a Road: An Autobiography* (Urbana: University of Illinois Press, 1984), 18.

24. For more on Heidegger's thinking about "having world," see his *The Fundamental Concepts of Metaphysics: World, Finitude, Solitude,* where he writes, "Man is not merely a part of the world but is also the master

and servant of the world in the sense of *having* world. Man has world. But then what about other beings which, like man, are also part of the world: the animals and plants, the material things like stone, for example? Are they merely parts of the world, as distinct from man who in addition *has* world? . . . However crudely, certain distinctions immediately manifest themselves here. We can formulate these distinctions in the following three theses: [1.] the stone (material object) is worldless, [2.] the animal is poor-in-the-world; [3.] the man is world-forming." Martin Heidegger, *The Fundamental Concepts of Metaphysics: World, Finitude, Solitude* (Bloomington: Indiana University Press, 1995), 176.

25. Hurston, *Their Eyes Were Watching God*, 93.
26. Sylvia Wynter, "Interview with Sylvia Wynter," *ProudFlesh: New Afrikan Journal of Culture, Politics & Consciousness* 4 (2006): 21.
27. Édouard Glissant, *Poetic Intention*, trans. Nathalie Stephens (Callicoon, NY: Nightboat, 2010), 18.
28. Ibid., 44.
29. Thomas Wentworth Higginson, "Negro Spirituals," *Atlantic*, June 1867.
30. Hurston, *Their Eyes Were Watching God*, 98.
31. Brian Massumi, *What Animals Teach Us about Politics* (Durham, NC: Duke University Press, 2014), 51.
32. Hurston, *Their Eyes Were Watching God*, 199.
33. Ibid., 200.
34. My use of the phrase "problem for thought" is a direct reference to Nahum Chandler's monograph *X: The Negro as a Problem for Thought* (New York: Fordham University Press, 2014).

4. Dog

Epigraphs: Patricia Smith, "Won't Be but a Minute," in *Blood Dazzler: Poems* (Minneapolis, MN: Coffee House Press, 2013), 10; DMX (Earl Simmons), "Dog Intro," track 1 on *Grand Champ* (Def Jam, 2003), compact disc.

1. See Michel Foucault, "Friendship as a Way of Life," in *Foucault Live: Interviews, 1966–1984*, ed. Sylvère Lotringer (New York: Semiotext(e), 1997), 207.
2. For more on entanglement, see Karen Barad, *Meeting the Universe Halfway: Quantum Physics and the Entanglement of Matter and Meaning* (Durham, NC: Duke University Press, 2007).

3. Carl Phillips, "White Dog," in *Quiver of Arrows: Selected Poems, 1986–2006* (New York: Macmillan, 2007), 172.

4. Jacob von Uexküll, "The Theory of Meaning," *Semiotica* 42, no. 1 (1982): 25–79.

5. Ibid., 27.

6. Camille T. Dungy, "Introduction: The Nature of African American Poetry," in *Black Nature: Four Centuries of African American Nature Poetry*, ed. Dungy (Athens: University of Georgia Press, 2009), xxiii.

7. Brian Hare and Vanessa Woods, *The Genius of Dogs: How Dogs Are Smarter than You Think* (New York: Penguin, 2013), 4.

8. Jesmyn Ward, *Salvage the Bones: A Novel* (New York: Bloomsbury, 2012), 8.

9. Ibid., 40.

10. Ibid., 77.

11. Ibid., 28.

12. Ibid., 121.

13. Colin Dayan, *With Dogs at the Edge of Life* (New York: Columbia University Press, 2015), xiii.

14. For more on the good life as I am referring to it here, see Lauren Berlant, *Cruel Optimism* (Durham, NC: Duke University Press, 2011).

15. Dayan, *With Dogs at the Edge of Life*, 10.

16. Ward, *Salvage the Bones*, 195.

17. Ibid., 194.

18. Ibid., 191.

19. See Malcolm Gladwell, "Troublemakers: What Pit Bulls Can Teach Us about Profiling," *New Yorker*, February 6, 2006, 38–43.

20. Ward, *Salvage the Bones*, 324.

21. Jacques Derrida, *Deconstruction in a Nutshell: A Conversation with Jacques Derrida*, ed. John D. Caputo (New York: Fordham University Press, 1997), 17; Fred Moten, "Black Op," *PMLA* 123, no. 5 (2008): 1746.

22. Ward, *Salvage the Bones*, 342.

23. See Samuel Beckett, *Watt* (New York: Faber and Faber, 2012), 249.

24. Ward, *Salvage the Bones*, 320.

25. See Giorgio Agamben, *The Open: Man and Animal* (Stanford, CA: Stanford University Press, 2004), 29.

26. Ibid., 351.

27. Ibid., 506, 507.

28. Ibid., 480.

29. Ibid., 513.

30. See Friedrich Nietzsche, *The Gay Science: With a Prelude in Rhymes and an Appendix of Songs* (New York: Vintage, 2010), 370–371.

31. "The Muck": Zora Neale Hurston, *Their Eyes Were Watching God: A Novel* (New York: Perennial Library, 1990); "The Clearing": Toni Morrison, *Beloved* (New York: Plume, 1988); "The Bottom": Toni Morrison, *Sula* (New York: Plume, 1982).

5. Shark

Epigraphs: William Bosman, *A New and Accurate Description of the Coast of Guinea: Divided into the Gold, the Slave, and the Ivory Coasts* (1705; repr., Cambridge: Cambridge University Press, 2011), 231–232; August Wilson, *Joe Turner's Come and Gone* (New York: Samuel French, Inc., 1990), 81; Hortense Spillers, "Mama's Baby, Papa's Maybe: An American Grammar Book," *Diacritics* 17, no. 2 (1987): 72.

1. See Saidiya Hartman, *Lose Your Mother: A Journey along the Atlantic Slave Route* (New York: Macmillan, 2008).

2. Camille Dungy, ed., *Black Nature: Four Centuries of African American Nature Poetry* (Athens: University of Georgia Press, 2009); Ian Frederick Finseth, *Shades of Green: Visions of Nature in the Literature of American Slavery, 1770–1860* (Athens: University of Georgia Press, 2009); Dianne D. Glave, *Rooted in the Earth: Reclaiming the African American Environmental Heritage* (Chicago: Chicago Review Press, 2010); Paul Outka, *Race and Nature from Transcendentalism to the Harlem Renaissance* (New York: Palgrave Macmillan, 2013).

3. See Sylvia Wynter, "Unsettling the Coloniality of Being / Power / Truth / Freedom: Towards the Human, after Man, Its Overrepresentation—An Argument," *CR: The New Centennial Review* 3, no. 3 (2008): 257.

4. Here, I am referring to the long cultural history that follows in the wake of the revolt, one that includes, of course, the Academy Award–nominated, 1997 Steven Spielberg film *Amistad*.

5. Robert Hayden, "Middle Passage," in *Collected Poems* (New York: Liveright, 2013), 48.

6. See Stephanie E. Smallwood, *Saltwater Slavery: A Middle Passage from Africa to American Diaspora* (Cambridge, MA: Harvard University Press, 2008), 122.

7. See Marcus Rediker, *Outlaws of the Atlantic: Sailors, Pirates, and Motley Crews in the Age of Sail* (Boston: Beacon, 2014), 195.

8. In the words of Thomas Clarkson in *Voyage to Guinea,* "It is an opinion, which the Africans universally entertain, that, as soon as death shall release them from the hands of their oppressors, they shall immediately be wafted back to their native plains, there to exist again, to enjoy the sight of their beloved countrymen, and to spend the while of their new existence in scenes of tranquility and delight: and so powerfully does this notion operate upon them, as to drive them frequently to the horrid extremity of putting a period to their lives." See Thomas Clarkson, *History of the Rise, Progress, and Accomplishment of the Abolition of the African Slave Trade by the British Parliament* (London: J. W. Parker, 1839), 155.

9. See Shawn O'Sullivan, "The Aquatic Invasion: A Drexciya Discography Review," *Exchange,* accessed August 12, 2016, http://ucexchange.uchicago .edu/reviews/aquatic.html.

10. See Sun Ra and His Solar Arkestra, *Atlantis,* MP3 (Saturn, 1967); Otolith Group, *Hydra Decapita,* 2010, http://otolithgroup.org/index.php ?m=project&id=3; Drexciya Research Lab, "Ellen Gallagher—Coral Cities," October 3, 2007, http://drexciyaresearchlab.blogspot.com/2007 /10/ellen-gallagher-coral-cities.html.

11. See Richard Iton, *In Search of the Black Fantastic: Politics and Popular Culture in the Post–Civil Rights Era* (Oxford: Oxford University Press, 2010).

12. See Stefano Harney and Fred Moten, *The Undercommons: Fugitive Planning & Black Study* (New York: Minor Compositions, 2013).

13. Hayden, "Middle Passage," 49.

14. See W. E. B. Du Bois, "The Souls of White Folk," in *Darkwater: Voices from within the Veil* (North Chelmsford, MA: Courier, 1920), 30.

15. Hayden, "Middle Passage," 54.

16. See Dipesh Chakrabarty, "The Climate of History: Four Theses," *Critical Inquiry* 35, no. 2 (2009): 197–222.

17. Marcus Rediker, "History from Below the Water Line: Sharks and the Atlantic Slave Trade," *Atlantic Studies* 5, no. 2 (2008): 285–297.

18. *The Black Power Mixtape 1967–1975: A Documentary in 9 Chapters,* directed by Göran Hugo Olsson (New York: Sundance Selects, 2011).

19. Melvin Beaunorus Tolson, "The Sea-Turtle and the Shark," *Negro American Literature Forum* 2, no. 2 (1968): 31.

20. Ibid.

21. Duke Franklin Humanities Institute, "The Black Outdoors: Fred Moten & Saidiya Hartman at Duke University," YouTube, October 5, 2016, https://www.youtube.com/watch?v=t_tUZ6dybrc.

22. This section's epigraph is from Rickey Laurentiis, "Mood for Love," in *Boy with Thorn* (Pittsburgh: University of Pittsburgh Press, 2015), 68. The phrase "had no selves to defend" comes from Mariame Kaba's writing, which can be found at www.usprisonculture.com; on her Twitter account, @prisonculture; and elsewhere.

23. Xandria Phillips, "For a Burial Free of Sharks," Gigantic Sequins, accessed August 12, 2016, http://www.giganticsequins.com/phillips81.html.

24. Monique Allewaert, *Ariel's Ecology: Plantations, Personhood, and Colonialism in the American Tropics* (Minneapolis: University of Minnesota Press, 2013), 3.

25. See Frantz Fanon, "The Fact of Blackness," in *Black Skin, White Masks* (New York: Grove, 2008), 113.

26. Vincent Brown, "Social Death and Political Life in the Study of Slavery," *American Historical Review* 114, no. 5 (2009): 1233.

27. Jonathan Howard, "The Soles of Black Folk: Blackness and the Lived Experience of Relation," *Esu Review*, 2016, http://www.esureview.org/content/academic-essays/the-soles-of-black-folk-blackness-and-the-lived-experience-of-relation-by-jonathan-howard/.

28. Phillips, "For a Burial Free of Sharks."

ACKNOWLEDGMENTS

I was raised within a tradition that emphasizes collective memory, the defense of the dead, and celebration in the face of unthinkable odds. This ongoing emphasis enters the world in many forms: the testimony, the ring shout, the shout-out, the altar call and street-corner altar for the slain, the naming of ancestors before any ceremony worth its salt can begin. So I want to close this work, my first book of literary theory, by invoking my great-grandmother Carrie, whose mother was born into the steel grip of chattel slavery near a town named for the man who claimed legal ownership of her and her kin, Lillington, and was somehow able to make a kind of life in spite of the brutal absurdity of this fact. I would like to dedicate this book to her and to my grandparents Charlotte and Levi, who met in a strawberry field 116 miles away from Lillington, in Wilmington, North Carolina. The central ideas undergirding this book bear the trace of the myriad forms of violence designed to circumscribe their lives, as well as the irreducible valor, and imagination, they cultivated in the midst of that terror. I am because they were, and are, and any good I accomplish is the result in no small part of their freedom dreams and prayer without ceasing.

All of which is to say, I cannot imagine the completion of this manuscript without the inimitable, invincible love of my family. Thank you, Toya, my big sister, my first friend and confidante and greatest supporter. Thank you, Mom and Dad, for the countless sacrifices that helped me arrive at this moment; for all that you gave and continue to give so that I might dedicate my life to language.

This book began as an idea in a first-year graduate seminar and was nurtured from that point onward by a group of advisers and mentors who have truly, at every turn, supported my growth as a writer and literary critic. To Imani Perry and Bill Gleason, thank you for taking me on as an energetic, wide-eyed twenty-two-year-old and helping hone my thinking around the black environmental imagination in its earliest stages. Imani, as you know better than anyone, I would not have made it to the point of this book's publication, or through graduate school at all, without your tenderness and commitment to seeing me through. It was a kindness I can never repay and will not soon forget.

A note of thanks as well to the incomparable Josef Sorett, who took on a graduate student from Princeton he had never met before as a TA for his Introduction to African American Studies course, ultimately welcoming him back to the city that raised him. The lessons I learned in that classroom were absolutely formative and continue to shape my pedagogical practice even now.

Thank you to Marc Lamont Hill, for giving me my first research job when I was still a sophomore in college. It meant more than you can know.

Thank you to all of the faculty and staff that played an integral role in getting me through the MMUF and SROP programs as an undergraduate—E. Patrick Johnson, Pat Ravenell, Thadious Davis, and John Jackson, among others—for your guidance and belief in my potential to change and grow.

Thank you to Gregory Pardlo for instructing me to "use all of [my] words" almost ten years ago, long before I had published a single word in anyone's literary journal.

Thank you to my friends. In so many ways, it was your abiding love and care that sustained me through the years and equipped me to think critically about the beauty and infinite possibilities of black social life: Thomas Alston, Jamil Baldwin, Kyle Brooks, Jamall Calloway, Devin Chamberlain, Daniel Claro, Ben Crossan, Jarvis Givens, Che Gossett, Elleza Kelley, Carvens Lissaint, Jesse McCarthy, Ernie Mitchell, Wesley Morris, Timothy Pantoja, Sherine Powerful, Rodney Reynolds, Jachele Velez, Jeremy Scott Vinson, and Everic White.

Thank you to the colleagues and interlocutors whose work has shaped my own approach to thinking the relationship between story and argument, style and form: La Marr Jurelle Bruce, Colin Dayan, Camille Dungy, Brigitte Fielder, Julius Fleming, James Haile, Saidiya Hartman, Zakkiyah

Jackson, Akira Lippit, Jarvis McInnis, Fred Moten, Tavia N'yongo, Sonya Posmentier, Elaine Scarry, Jared Sexton, Christina Sharpe, Hortense Spillers, and Brandon Terry.

Thank you to Professor Sylvia Wynter for your world-shifting work, as well as for the January 2019 conversation that changed the way I think about the stakes and aims of scholarship *as such*.

To all my colleagues at the Harvard Society of Fellows, thank you for the conversations that helped me put the final touches on this book and get it out into the world. You all stretched my thinking in ways that were absolutely integral to the present and future of this broader research project.

Much of *Shark* was published in 2018 as "Beyond the Vomiting Dark: Toward a Black Hydropoetics" in *Ecopoetics: Essays in the Field*, edited by Angela Hume and Gillian Osborne, and is reprinted here by permission of University of Iowa Press.

Thank you to my editor, Sharmila Sen, for reminding me, from our very first conversation, to write from a place of conviction and radical honesty.

Thank you to Cornel West for the inspiration, when I was seventeen years old, not only to become a professor but to major in something called "African American Studies," based on the bio I read on the back of his classic monograph, *Race Matters*.

Thank you to the Ford Foundation, the Josephine De Karman Fellowship Trust, the Milton Fund at Harvard University, the School of Humanities, Arts, and Social Sciences at MIT, and the Graduate School at Princeton University for their generous support of this research from its earliest stages.

Thank you to my colleagues at Dartmouth College for welcoming me into the profession and for supporting me through the final stages of completing this manuscript.

And, finally, thank you to the countless strangers, readers, and listeners, online and elsewhere, who ever said a kind word, watched a video, or purchased a ticket to one of my readings. From the time I was a teenager, you helped instill in me the confidence that I could take this writing in any direction I desired and that there might actually be someone on the other end willing to engage it in good faith. Wherever you are, wherever you are headed, thank you for holding my words precious. It made all the difference.

INDEX